La Dolce Vita

La Dolce Vita

SWEET DREAMS & CHOCOLATE MEMORIES

Isabel Coe

SIMON & SCHUSTER

A VIACOM COMPANY

First published by Simon & Schuster UK Ltd, 2005
A Viacom Company

Copyright © Isabel Coe, 2005

Simon & Schuster UK Ltd
Africa House
64–78 Kingsway
London WC2B 6AH

1 3 5 7 9 10 8 6 4 2

Designer: *Fiona Andreanelli*
Line illustrations: *Isabel Coe* (unless otherwise indicated)
Copy editor: *Nicole Foster*
Proofreaders: *Nicole Foster, Anne Doggett*
Indexer: *Anne Doggett*

Printed and bound in Italy

ISBN 0 74326 845 8

For my mother – for love, inspiration and a magical childhood.

Special thanks to Al, Indy and Minnie – where would I be without you and your tireless enthusiasm for everything I do?

Acknowledgements

Enormous thanks to my father, my brother Jem, and to my family all over the world, without whom this book would never have been possible – thank you for sharing your memories and unlocking the delicious secrets of the past; to Maggie and Mike for your huge support and filling my home with chocolate books; to Em, Jools and Naomi for food tasting and chocolatey girls' nights in, and to Howard, Clara and Jane D for showing me that this was possible. Enormous thanks also to Kim, Nicole and Fiona at Martin Books for guiding me through this process and continuous support and encouragement, and to Janet Copleston for believing in me.

Contents

Introduction

Wherever I've been, whatever I've been doing, chocolate is never far from my mind. Chewy, warm Weinacht Guezi at Christmas; rich chocolatey Napoleon's Torte on my birthday; chocolate truffles on St Nicholas's Day – my mother made them all and it would be impossible to pick a favourite – each one harboured its own, special memory and made distant family seem closer.

Now that I am a mother myself, those memories are flooding back. It is as though the ancient spell of one of the world's most enchanting ingredients is bringing the past to life and filling my home with the sweet aroma of vanilla and cocoa.

All food has its own magic, but with chocolate there is also an intangible quality, a chemistry which can cure even the worst case of distemper. There is something in the alchemy of melting, mixing and grating it which sets it apart from other forms of cooking and makes eating it an unrivalled pleasure.

My mother taught me that alchemy when I was barely old enough to reach the mixing bowl, just as her mother and grandmother had opened her eyes to the joy of cooking and the pleasure of good food when she was a girl. I still remember the smooth gloss on a bowl of her perfectly tempered couverture and my wide-eyed wonder at how she could turn the gooey mixture in the cake tin into something so warm and inviting. I thought there was some wonderful secret to it all and hoped, even then, that she would teach it to me some day.

Being a small part of a very large Italian family, I was brought up to enjoy cooking and, over the years, the joy of sharing good food with family and friends has become a way of life. But of all our family's culinary pleasures, chocolate has long been a favourite. Somehow there was an unspoken understanding that it was the noblest of all ingredients – a thing to be savoured. I often watched as my schoolfriends spent their pocket money on sweets and sugary chocolate bars and felt a little smug that my own mother would spare us those tooth-rotting confections in favour of a small, delicious home-made biscuit or cake. In this way, my brother Jem and I were taught to savour the good and avoid the bad. It is a lesson I have remembered over the years and intend to repeat with my own children, a lesson my mother learnt when she was growing up in post-war Italy where treats were scarce but always gratefully appreciated.

I suppose that in many ways, chocolate was our 'chicken soup', our 'tea and biscuits': it was what we relied on to spice up festive occasions and celebrations, what I knew I would be treated to if I had done well at school and what we were given to fight both winter colds and broken hearts.

I still remember waking up to the smell of cocoa and cinnamon on the first Saturday in December, and going into the kitchen to see my mother preparing the dough for her Omama's Christmas Guezi. As she grated the chocolate and rolled the mix into fat sausages, ready to chill overnight, she would tell me stories of her grandmother, Omama, who always had a batch of these special biscuits ready when she arrived in Switzerland for the winter holidays. I would go to bed that night with a warm feeling in my stomach and thoughts of my mother as a little girl swirling happily around my head. Though perhaps the best of all my chocolate memories are my mother's chocolate sandwiches – made with thin slabs of dark, Menier cooking chocolate and slices of crusty white bread.

But whatever she was making, whether it was Omama's Chocolate Mousse or Nonna's chestnut truffles, it was the knowledge that her own family – dispersed all over Switzerland and Italy – were doing the same thing in their kitchens that made cooking not just a delight but a necessity for my mother. Those treasured recipes were all she had when she arrived in London, and the sweet scent they released was like a warm embrace on a cold day in a city so far from home. It is the same for me now, embarking on a new life in Australia with only these edible hand-me-downs and my blissful childhood memories for comfort from the ever-present homesickness.

It is certainly no coincidence that most, if not all, of my fondest memories of growing up involve food. I was raised on Italian traditions and the best of all of these is the importance of the kitchen. *La cucina* is the heart of the home, a place where families and friends come together to eat, chat and cook. I rarely spent any time in my bedroom when I was a child, preferring instead to do my homework at the kitchen table while my mother prepared dinner. She would hand me a thick hunk of rind from the Parmesan as she grated some for our spaghetti or the leftover chocolate mousse from the mixing bowl once she had filled all the pots. I made my Christmas cards there when I was little, with a mug of hot cocoa and a dish of my mother's chocolate sandwiches. It was in the kitchen that I studied for my school exams, with a chocolate espresso to wake me up. And it was there that my mother taught me about my ancestry – armed with chocolate dishes which have been passed down through four generations of women in my family.

I learnt to cook when I was old enough to enjoy food, and one of the most valuable lessons my mother taught me was to improvise – to put my trust, as she had done, in the quality of my ingredients. Watching her at work, adding a little of this, a pinch of that, never following a recipe to the letter, taught me not to be afraid to try new things. So if you find yourself making a batch of chocolate-drizzled Breton biscuits or a rich ganache Torte and can't remember the exact ingredients, do add a little of this or a pinch of that, and let yourself be guided by the beautiful simplicity of chocolate.

Buon Appetito!

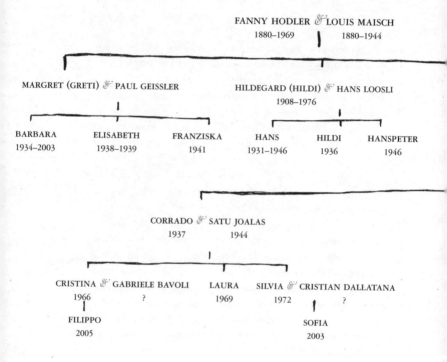

FANNY HODLER & LOUIS MAISCH
1880–1969   1880–1944

MARGRET (GRETI) & PAUL GEISSLER

BARBARA   ELISABETH   FRANZISKA
1934–2003   1938–1939   1941

HILDEGARD (HILDI) & HANS LOOSLI
1908–1976

HANS   HILDI   HANSPETER
1931–1946   1936   1946

CORRADO & SATU JOALAS
1937   1944

CRISTINA & GABRIELE BAVOLI   LAURA   SILVIA & CRISTIAN DALLATANA
1966   ?   1969   1972   ?

FILIPPO   SOFIA
2005   2003

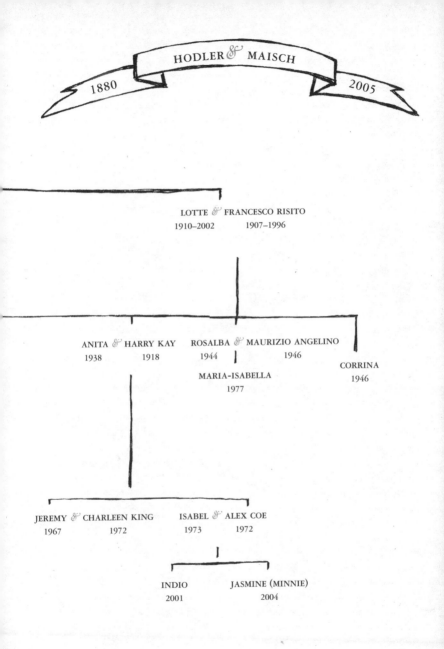

HODLER & MAISCH
1880   2005

LOTTE & FRANCESCO RISITO
1910–2002   1907–1996

ANITA & HARRY KAY   ROSALBA & MAURIZIO ANGELINO
1938   1918   1944   1946
                                                              CORRINA
                           MARIA-ISABELLA   1946
                           1977

JEREMY & CHARLEEN KING   ISABEL & ALEX COE
1967   1972   1973   1972

INDIO   JASMINE (MINNIE)
2001   2004

PART ONE:

Sweet Dreams

I discovered that she had Nonno's eyes – deep, earnest pools of chocolate brown – and Nonna's hearty, beautiful smile, and that she shares my cousin Silvia's natural talent for life. It is a strange and wonderful luxury to have your family tree – old photographs, toys, clothes, books – all under one roof. But that's what Schonortli was like – a living, breathing memory-box – rather like opening the door to a dusty old attic and being dazzled by a rainbow of colours from the past.

But of all the places there were to play and hide, it was always in the small, rustic kitchen that I felt most at home, comforted by the warmth of the stove and the promise of something sweet inside. As my mother and aunts cooked in there, their happy chattering like the pulse which ran through the old house, I wanted more than anything to be like them. I watched, hungry to learn, as they grated ice-cold butter into the pastry dough for our favourite fruit Kuchen and fell respectfully silent when my mother broke pieces of black Lindt Excellence into a bowl and melted them down slowly, with love. Now she berates me if I boil the water in my bain-marie, telling me that the heat will spoil the gloss. I suppose, as children, that was why we all loved chocolate so much – everything else was always done with frantic speed on those holidays but chocolate, with its noble arrogance, would not be rushed, and it bought us some precious time with our parents.

When Opapa bought the house, he was already a successful lawyer with another beautiful home in the heart of Berne. But he had worked hard for everything he owned, looking after his ailing mother during the day and studying for his Bar exams at night.

Omama shared his keen mind and strong work ethic, having taken a job as governess to a little English girl called Gladys when she was just 17. She later told my mother that she had saved enough money from the post to travel, unchaperoned, to London, where she bought a tailored blue suit at Selfridges and watched Queen Victoria parade through the city in a horse-drawn carriage.

But, unlike Opapa, hers had been a privileged childhood. Her father was the renowned Bernese architect Alfred Hodler, who designed many of the buildings in the city's historic centre. He doted on his daughter and thought she had such a timeless beauty that he used her face as the template for the figure of Switzerland on the city's university building. The statue faces Berne's main railway station, and it is a source of great family pride that anyone visiting for the first time will see Omama's face as they step outside. Her cousin was the world-famous Art Nouveau painter Ferdinand Hodler, whose dark, sombre canvases adorned the walls in Schonortli's *salotto* for many years, and her brother, Walter, married into the prestigious Della Casa family. His wife's niece was the popular Swiss soprano Lisa Della Casa and, when my mother was a

girl, Nonna and Nonno went to see her sing in *Der Rosenkavalier* at Milan's La Scala. They brought back a signed black and white photograph of her in which she looks like a young Elizabeth Taylor, and they said that her voice had brought tears to their eyes.

My mother as a young girl with a relative. Uncle Walter and Omama

Omama loved music too and was already an accomplished pianist by the time she met Opapa. She had dreams of hosting wonderful dinner parties for his friends and entertaining them with her recitals. But for that, she needed to learn to cook. She was, my mother tells me, a lady who liked to do things properly and before she and Opapa got married, she enrolled herself in a cookery course in Berne – working on the healthy assumption that good food is the best way to a man's heart.

Lisa Della Casa

She bought herself a green note-book with the words '*Meine Kochrezepte*' (my recipes) written on the front and started copying down everything she learnt. Years later, when she was more confident of her skills, she bought a traditional French cookery book which came with a few sheets of lined paper in the back. There, she wrote all her menu ideas for those excellent soirées she had so looked forward to having.

LISA DELLA CASA

DECCA

After she and Opapa were married, they employed a cook to prepare their everyday meals, but when they entertained, Omama insisted on doing everything herself. My mother tells me, with granddaughterly pride, that she became quite well known for her saddle of venison and chateaubriand, but it was her desserts which won her the most praise. She would bake chocolate madeleines and serve them with Crème Chocolat for summer dinners in the garden and her chocolate mousse – made only with whipping cream and grated Lindt – has since been passed down from Nonna to my mother and from her to me.

Traditions are important to any family and in mine, they always come with chocolate

Like my mother, she always cooked with passion and joy, but it was at Christmas that she really excelled herself. Traditions are important to any family and in mine, they always come with chocolate – chocolate spice biscuits to eat on Christmas Eve, chocolate-coated star biscuits for the tree, chocolate Lebkuchen and rich chocolate truffles for St Nicholas's Day. Even Nonna, who was not a natural cook, knew that no Christmas was complete without these delicacies and my mother has fond memories of her mother – flour in her hair and chocolate on her apron – cutting shapes in Omama's Vanillepretzel and coating them with a kirsch glaze.

Omama saw that her youngest daughter had an appreciation of sweet things and, when she was old enough, she enrolled her in a dessert course in Berne – hoping that a little tempering might make a domestic creature of her. I have often thought that my nonna must have been quite a rare breed in her day – a woman with four children and a food-loving Italian husband to feed at a time when money was scarce, who had only one culinary string to her bow – a course in Swiss cake-making.

Born in Berne in 1907, Nonna – little Lotti Maisch – was the youngest of three sisters, the blonde-haired, blue-eyed apple of her father's eye. All three: Lotti, Hildi, the middle sister, and Greti, the eldest – a raven-haired beauty who went on to become an excellent lawyer like her father – were headstrong, intelligent women, but it was Nonna who always looked the happiest in old family photographs.

Despite her fine features and feminine good looks, she was a bit of a tomboy at heart, so it came as a real surprise to her to

2 Eßlöffel Wasser. Die zerbröckelte Schokolade mit dem Wasser auf
kleinem Feuer auflösen. Glatt rühren, die Butter und das
gut verklopfte Ei zufügen. Die Biscuits mit dieser
Masse überziehen. Je 3–4 nebeneinander auf eine Platte
legen, ebensoviele quer darüber und so fort, bis das Ganze
die Größe eines Pflastersteins hat. Mit dem Rest der Creme
überziehen. Wenn möglich einige Stunden kühl stellen,
und es 2 od. beide gezuckerten Schlagrahm ausgarnieren.

Basler Bruns (...)

4 Eiweiss, 2 Eßlöffel Kirsch, 200 gr Zucker, 250 gr geriebene Schokolade,
500 g ungeschälte, geriebene Haselnüsse (oder Mandeln) (...)
Alles zu einem kleinen Teig und einen gelben klebrigen Teig kneten
... mit Zucker fermentenen Teigs ½ cm dick ausrollen, mit Gläser
ausstechen, etwas trocknen lassen. Im zuführen 10 Min. etwa bei
150–200°. ...

Buttercreme

1. Art   ½ dl Wasser, ...
            einkochen. Über ...
Weiterrühren bis zum Erk...
Rühren in 120–150 g ...
nach Belieben etwas Rhum...
Schokolade zufügen. ...
Stelle von ½ dl Wasser eb...

3/4 dl Wasser, 420 gr Zucker, 4 g...

Omama's recipe book

Meine
Kochrezepte

discover that she actually liked learning how to make rich chocolate brownies and chocolate Tortes with shiny glazes; making cakes and sweets was to be the only culinary activity she truly enjoyed, finding it both relaxing and fun. She delighted in rolling her Truffes aux Marrons in bitter cocoa powder, or coating them with a white chocolate icing, and took great pride in knowing how to decorate them with delicate chocolate ribbons. I have only ever made these once – with my mother. We put them in little boxes and gave them away as gifts, enjoying the closeness of making something so special together and the image of Nonna doing the same thing many years before us.

Nonna's first home in Berne

TRUFFES AUX MARRONS – NONNA'S ELEGANT CHESTNUT TRUFFLES

150 g (5½ oz) dark chocolate
75 g (2¾ oz) unsalted butter
1 tablespoon milk
370 g (13 oz) sweet chestnut purée
1 egg yolk
1 teaspoon dark rum
icing sugar and cocoa powder for coating

Melt the chocolate and stir in the butter until it has dissolved, then mix in the rest of the ingredients to form a soft dough.

Wrap the mixture in clingfilm and store in the refrigerator for at least 8 hours.

When you're ready to use it, roll tiny amounts at a time into longish, monkey-nut shaped truffles, about 3 cm (1¼ inches) by 0.5 cm (¼ inch) and roll some in icing sugar and some in bitter cocoa powder.

(For a really special occasion, melt equal quantities of dark and white chocolate. Dip some of the truffles in the dark chocolate and drizzle the white chocolate on top in thin strips.)

Makes about 25

Once she had mastered the basics, Nonna went on to try out Omama's old recipes. She trawled through her mother's worn green notebook for things to practise on, and with a steady hand and an ordered mind she started at the beginning, with Basler Brauns – a traditional Swiss recipe for chocolate brownies made with kirsch and Lindt cooking chocolate. I serve these on stormy autumn days with a jug of fresh pouring cream, and smile at the image of Nonna abandoning her usual uncreased elegance in favour of chocolatey hands and a sticky mixing bowl.

BASLER BRAUNS –
FROM OMAMA'S RECIPE BOOK

4 egg whites, whisked until stiff
2 tablespoons kirsch
200 g (7 oz) caster sugar
250 g (9 oz) grated chocolate
    (Lindt Excellence or Menier)
500 g (1 lb 2 oz) ground unpeeled hazelnuts or almonds

Mix everything in a blender for 3 minutes, or a little longer by hand.

Shape the mixture into a long roll, then dust a baking tray with sugar and roll the mixture out in it until it is about 3–4 cm (1¹/₂ inches) thick. Score into small squares and refrigerate overnight.

Next day, bake at Gas Mark 6/200°C/fan oven 180°C for about 10 minutes – the brownies must be chewy when they come out.

Eat warm with fresh, ice-cold cream.

Makes about 10

Next in the book was Omama's recipe for Honigleckerli – a spiced honey bread, a little like Lebekuchen, which we make to eat with Glühwein on Christmas Eve. There is no chocolate in this recipe, but it's so delicious I feel it deserves a mention – you can always cut it into stars and pipe some dark chocolate around the edges for a Christmas tree decoration.

HONIGLECKERLI: MAMIS REZEPT – HONEY SPICE BREAD: MUMMY'S RECIPE

250 g (9 oz) ground unpeeled hazelnuts
250 g (9 oz) whole blanched almonds
500 g (1 lb 2 oz) caster sugar
30 g (1¼ oz) plain flour
100 g (3½ oz) candied orange peel
a pinch of cinnamon
2 tablespoons kirsch
2–3 tablespoons clear honey
3 egg whites
200 g (7 oz) icing sugar

Preheat the oven to Gas Mark 3/160°C/fan oven 140°C.

Mix all the ingredients apart from the icing sugar together vigorously until they form a dough.

Roll out the dough on a sugared work surface to about 1 cm (½ inch) thick and cut into shapes of your choosing.

Bake for 10 minutes and then increase the temperature to Gas Mark 4/ 180°C/fan oven 160°C and bake for a further 10 minutes.

Make a sugar syrup by mixing the icing sugar with 4 tablespoons water and use it to glaze the Honigleckerli while still warm.

Nonna and Nonno The book proved to be a treasure-chest of delights, but despite upholding the family tradition of sweet-making, Nonna hated to be tied to the kitchen. Instead, she followed in Omama's independent footsteps and did well at school, winning a place at Berne university to study literature before taking a year out to study at Florence university. She hoped the experience would give her a greater understanding of the country's culture and the city's glorious art works. But she came away with a little more than she had bargained for, as it was there, at an after-class tennis club, that she met Nonno.

Physically, they were strikingly different. He had the dark, brooding looks of a young Valentino, whilst hers was the milky-white beauty he had only ever seen in films at the cinema where as a little boy he worked as an usher, staring transfixed at the big screen and wondering if such exotic creatures actually existed. Well now he knew they did and he fell head-over-heels in love, vowing to finish his studies and provide her with the fine lifestyle he knew she deserved.

Nonna, who had been brought up a Protestant, soon converted and they were married four years later in a little Catholic church in Berne. Opapa instantly welcomed Nonno into his family, seeing something of himself in the earnest, industrious young man who

had won his daughter's heart. Like Opapa, Nonno had been working hard during the day to pay his way through university, studying for his accountancy exams at night.

Nonna and Nonno on their wedding day

His parents, Argia and Ernesto Risito, were poor, unsophisticated people who had met as teenagers when she was working as a cook and he as a stable boy for a wealthy family in the countryside near Florence. After the First World War, Ernesto moved to the city to open a *tabaccheria* – Il Tredici Rosso – which Nonno and his younger brother Enrico helped run while they were still at home.

Nonno was one of six children, but sadly the eldest, Francesco, died before Nonno was born and his sister Paola died of typhoid when she was 18. He had another sister, Marcella, who had a soft spot for my mother. She always loved dancing and had fantasised about becoming an acrobat and joining the circus. She probably would have done if it hadn't been for her mother's refusal to let her travel the country with a group of loose-living gypsies! Instead, she took up needlework and used to embroider linen for young women as wedding presents. She fell hopelessly in love with a dashing, young horse-riding instructor when she was still a teenager, but by then, her mother was ill with arthritis and confined to a wheelchair, so she turned down his offer of marriage to stay at home and nurse her. Being a passionate, headstrong Italian, he refused to give up and when her mother died, many years later, he proposed again. By then Marcella was already in her fifties, but she accepted and they had a devoted and happy marriage. She died before him and my mother tells me that he was so besotted with her, he would visit her grave every day with a fresh, red rose.

Nonno was very close to his family and would never have dreamed of moving to Switzerland while his parents were still alive, so instead Nonna moved to be with him. Life in Milan would be many things over the years – tense, difficult, hot – but at first it was just lonely. She missed her family and the crisp, mountain air of home, but she soon learnt the same lesson my mother learnt when she left her home and I am learning now – that cooking family recipes makes the pain of separation more bearable. It fills your home with familiar smells and your tummy

Zia Marcella's husband

with a satisfying fullness which wards off the sad longing for home for a few, abandoned moments.

Soon after they were married, my Uncle Corrado was born and, a year later, my mother came along. Nonna, once a proud and independent young woman, was fast becoming a 'Hausfrau' with a growing family to feed, and Omama's recipes never failed her. She baked Christmas biscuits in the heat in Milan; she made Hernli, a Swiss version of macaroni cheese, when the children were little; and she even converted Nonno to fondues. But her favourite family recipe was one she found in Omama's green book – Crème Chocolat. She thought it sounded terribly refined and, when my mother was older, used to make endless variations of it for friends when she and Nonno hosted their regular bridge evenings. Nonno, who was brought up on his mother's traditional Italian cooking, hated these sugary cream desserts: 'It is not Italian,' he would shout in his hot,

Nonno, who was brought up on his mother's traditional Italian cooking, hated these sugary cream desserts: 'It is not Italian'

booming voice. 'In Italy, we do not eat creams.' But she made them none the less and annotated each recipe in her book with comments like '*Zehr gut*' (very good), and when she had made one she was particularly pleased with – 'Fine'!

The 'bridge set' were a discerning lot and Nonna loved to impress them with her recipe for a rather potent strawberry punch. She would prepare it early in the morning, pouring champagne and rum over a bowl of wild mountain strawberries, slowly adding more alcohol through the day. Nonno was in charge of serving it, but one hot summer's night he got a terrible shock. When he went to top up the glasses, he saw that they were out of wine, even though the evening was still young. So he took the punch bowl into the kitchen and added some sparkling water instead, sure they would never spot the difference. But just at that moment the earth shook with alarming force. It was only one of the minor earthquakes which are common in Italy in summer, but Nonno, a devout Catholic, was sure that God was punishing him for watering down the drinks. Terrified, he poured the whole lot down the sink and returned to his friends with his tail between his legs and a humble confession.

Nonna made Omama's Crème Chocolat the lazy way, not even whipping the cream first, so that she ended up with a rather insipid sweet soup. But Omama's crème was an 'intelligent' dessert – one that tastes rich yet is somehow light to eat – and the perfect accompaniment to a dish of her chocolate madeleines.

OMAMA'S CRÈME CHOCOLAT

300 ml (10 fl oz) double cream
1 vanilla pod, split lengthways
1 ½ tablespoons boiling water
150 g (5½ oz) dark chocolate
2 tablespoons caster sugar

Place the cream in a bowl with the vanilla pod and leave to infuse.

Pour the boiling water over the chocolate and stir until dissolved. Stir in the sugar and leave to cool.

Lightly whip the cream and fold into the chocolate mixture.

Eat slowly and savour every mouthful.

Serves 8 generously

Sadly, Nonna and Nonno didn't have much time together before war began to loom. It was clear that Mussolini was leading his country along a path to certain destruction and Omama and Opapa begged Nonna and the children to come and live with them in Berne until it was over. But it wasn't that simple, and the years ahead would be filled with danger and a sadness and loneliness that robbed my mother and Corrado of a part of their childhoods.

CHAPTER 2:

Escape from Milan

Nonno – desperate to keep his young family together – resisted sending Nonna and the children to Switzerland as long as he could. But once the war started and the bombings began, it became clear that Milan was no longer a safe place to live.

Omama and Opapa sent food parcels as often as they could, and they would always include tins of plain oat biscuits and slabs of Nestlé condensed milk. Nonna would tell my mother and Corrado that these fudge-like bars were the best white chocolate in the world and to be eaten slowly. Chocolate itself was an extremely rare commodity in those days and for my mother, the 'white chocolate' from her Omama was like a small taste of heaven, and she would go to bed that night dreaming of mountains and fresh clean air.

My mother,
age three
Uncle Corrado,
age four

It wasn't long before the air attacks on Milan got a little too close to home. My mother still remembers one incident clearly. Nonno had taken her and Corrado into the city to run some errands for Nonna, who was ill in bed with flu. My mother was only three and a half at the time and remembers gripping tightly on to their father's hand as he weaved in and out of the morning crowds. Suddenly they felt a tremor followed by a loud, crashing sound. Before they had time to panic, Nonno had scooped them up, my mother under one arm, Corrado under the other and like this he ran through the streets, never once stopping until he reached home. That was their first experience of a daytime raid. What my mother remembers most is dangling, upside down, under her father's arm, looking across at her brother and wondering if the world was about to end.

They had had a lucky escape, but Nonna and Nonno knew the time had come to take steps to ensure their children would be safe. Opapa's home in Berne was far too big for just the two of them and he insisted it would be better for everyone if they came and stayed, just until things settled down. No one knew how long the war would last, but Nonno, like every other able-bodied man at the time, had commitments in the army and to leave then would have been a very serious offence. In addition he had a good job, which he could not afford to risk leaving. They deliberated for as long as they could, but the bombs were getting closer and in the summer of 1943 it was decided that Nonna would leave with my mother and Corrado. It was the hardest decision of her life – she longed to escape to the security of her parents' home, where she knew her two little ones would be safe, but at the same time, she hated the thought of leaving Nonno behind.

The journey ahead would be a gruelling and dangerous one: it was an eight-hour trek over the Monte Moro mountains into Brig and no one had attempted such a daring escape before. Nonna had grown up on mountain walks but even she was nervous of undertaking such a long trip with two small children. Their escape had to be planned meticulously – if they were caught, they risked losing everything.

It was the hardest decision of her life – she longed to escape to the security of her parents' home, where she knew her two little ones would be safe, but at the same time, she hated the thought of leaving Nonno behind

My mother remembers that that summer they took a short holiday near Bellinzona, close to the start of the mountain pass. It was one of the happiest memories of her early childhood: Nonno had been working long hours for so long that it was a rare treat to have the whole family together. But nevertheless the holiday was filled with tension. Nonna knew she didn't have long to prepare for her ordeal and every morning she would take my mother and Corrado on a brisk walk, a little longer each time, to build up their strength for the task ahead.

Finally the time had come. They picked a dark evening towards the end of August, leaving with two mountain guides and a large picnic rucksack. Nonno accompanied them on the first leg of their journey – a four-hour hike, at the end of which my mother was exhausted and tearful. They sang Italian marching songs to keep them going but it was still an arduous walk, especially as they had just discovered that Nonna was pregnant and unable to carry either of the children for long.

As they approached the top of the mountain, their guides warned them that there would be two huts. One would be empty, the other would house some sleeping guards. They needed to stop and eat something if they were going to have enough strength for the downward journey, but no one knew which hut was which. An agonising moment passed while they made their decision. Thankfully it was the right one and Nonna told her children to sit quietly as she opened her rucksack and gave them each a hard-boiled egg and a block of Omama's 'white chocolate'. The guides cooked some mountain risotto and they shared a sombre meal together.

Before long she was in tears, but Nonna couldn't risk waking the guards in the other hut and shouted at her to be quiet.

My mother remembers having mixed feelings that night: on the one hand she was excited at being allowed a midnight snack, on the other she was tired and wanted nothing more than her soft warm bed. Before long she was in tears, but Nonna couldn't risk waking the guards in the other hut and shouted at her to be quiet. It was the first time Nonna had let her anxiety show and my mother remembers feeling hurt and confused, but it worked and she ate the rest of her meal in silence.

It was at this halfway point that Nonna had to say goodbye to Nonno, not knowing if she would ever see him alive again, at the same time trying to keep her spirits up for my mother and Corrado. My mother still remembers the expression on her face – the heartache of a woman who desperately wanted to cling to her husband, but knew she must be brave for her children.

Nonno in the mountains

*Nonna with Corrado
and my mother.
Bellinzona 1943*

*Nonno with Corrado
and my mother.
Bellinzona 1943*

The path down was a little easier – it was getting lighter and my mother was even given a hard fruit sweet by one of the guides, but as they approached the border with Brig at the bottom of the mountain they saw some soldiers. Nonna raised her arms high in the air and shouted to them that she was a Swiss national. There was an eerie moment's silence and then one of the soldiers came running towards them. He had been at school with her and when he saw how exhausted they were he offered to carry my mother the rest of the way.

They had made it, just as daylight was creeping through the clouds, and that's when my mother – tired and irritable – saw Opapa. When she tells the story now, she says she remembers everything about how he looked. His white hair was combed to one side and he was wearing a tweed jacket and wool trousers. His arms outstretched, tears in his eyes and a broad smile on his face, he rushed over and gave them all a warm, emotional embrace. Then, slowly, he dipped his hands into his jacket pockets and came out with two brightly wrapped chocolate sticks. They were Cailler praline bars; one was shiny blue, the other shiny red.

My mother unwrapped hers carefully and tasted the milky chocolate with caution. It was like nothing she had ever had before. Suddenly she realised the 'white chocolate' she had loved so much from her omama's food parcels hadn't been real chocolate at all – not like this. The bar was creamy and melted in her mouth. The nuts were crisp and she could taste the rich milk she had dreamed of in her bedroom back home in Milan. Both she and Corrado saved their wrappers for months to come, taking them out each time they wanted to remember the taste of their first chocolate bar.

We still buy those praline bars each time we go to Switzerland, but you can make them just as easily at home. It is a lovely idea to wrap them in bright paper like the original ones and hide them in the garden for a special Easter treat. I like making them with creamy milk chocolate and croccante (caramelised almonds), but you can make excellent after-dinner ones with dark chocolate and caramelised hazelnuts instead.

MILK CHOCOLATE PRALINE FINGERS

For the croccante (praline)
70 g (2³/₄ oz) caster sugar
200 g (7 oz) blanched almonds
For the chocolate truffle
250 ml (9 fl oz) double cream
400 g (14 oz) milk chocolate
2 tablespoons slightly salted butter

To make the croccante, bring the sugar and 3 tablespoons of water to the boil over a high heat. Stir well until the colour starts to turn a deep caramel. Add the almonds and stir with a wooden spoon until they are all coated in the sugar syrup.

Turn the mixture on to a lightly buttered baking tray or sheet of baking parchment and leave to cool.

Meanwhile, bring the cream to the boil in a saucepan. Remove from the heat and pour over the chocolate, stirring until it has all melted. Return the mixture to the pan, add the butter and stir slowly over a medium heat.

Crush the croccante well with a rolling pin, and add them to the chocolate truffle mix.

Stir it all together and place in a bowl in the refrigerator for several hours until it has solidified.

To shape the praline fingers, take a large spoonful at a time and roll it into a thin sausage. Cut into fingers roughly 2.5 cm (1 inch) in length.

Wrap each one first in a sheet of foil paper and then in a strip of coloured gift wrap, twisting the ends for an attractive finish.

Makes about 35

When we used to have these praline fingers on picnics in the mountains, my mother would sing us the same Partisan marching song she sang with her parents during her escape.

Bella Ciao

Una mattina, mi son svegliata,
Oh bella ciao, bella ciao,
Bella ciao, ciao, ciao,
Una mattina, mi son svegliata,
Ed ho trovato l'invasor

Oh partigiano, portami via,
Oh bella ciao, bella ciao,
Bella ciao, ciao, ciao,
Oh partigiano, portami via,
Che mi sento di morir

E se io muoio, da partigiano,
Oh bella ciao, bella ciao,
Bella ciao, ciao, ciao,
E se io muoio, da partigiano,
U mi devi seppellir

Seppellire lassù, in montagna
Oh bella ciao, bella ciao,
Bella ciao, ciao, ciao,
Seppellire lassù, in montagna
Sotto l'ombra di un bel fior

E tutti quelli, che passeranno
Oh bella ciao, bella ciao,
Bella ciao, ciao, ciao,
E tutti quelli, che passeranno
Diranno guarda che bel fior

E bello il fiore, del partigiano
Oh bella ciao, bella ciao,
Bella ciao, ciao, ciao,
E bello il fiore, del partigiano
Morto per la liberta.

Goodbye beautiful one
One morning, I woke up,
Oh goodbye beautiful one, goodbye beautiful one,
beautiful one goodbye, goodbye, goodbye
One morning, I woke up
And I found an intruder

Oh Partisan, carry me away
Oh goodbye beautiful one, goodbye beautiful one,
beautiful one goodbye, goodbye, goodbye
Oh Partisan, carry me away
because I feel like I am dying

And if I die as a Partisan
Oh goodbye beautiful one, goodbye beautiful one,
beautiful one goodbye, goodbye, goodbye
And if I die as a Partisan,
Then you must bury me

Bury me up in the mountain,
Oh goodbye beautiful one, goodbye beautiful one,
beautiful one goodbye, goodbye, goodbye
Bury me up in the mountain
Under the shade of a beautiful flower

And everyone who shall pass
Oh goodbye beautiful one, goodbye beautiful one,
beautiful one goodbye, goodbye, goodbye
And everyone who shall pass
Will say what a beautiful flower it is

The flower of the Partisan is beautiful
Oh goodbye beautiful one, goodbye beautiful one,
beautiful one goodbye, goodbye, goodbye
The flower of the Partisan is beautiful
It is the flower of freedom.

CHAPTER 3:

Festive Delights

*L*ife after their daring escape seemed fun at first – the family had even made the headlines as the first to make it over the mountain pass to the safety of neutral Switzerland, and their bravery paved the way for others to do the same. But before long the novelty started to wear off and my mother yearned to return home to her father and friends. It was late August 1943 – Nonna was a few weeks pregnant with my aunt Rosalba, my mother was just about to turn five and Corrado was six. If they had been in Milan, the children would have been sharing one room, but Opapa's home in Berne was a beautiful old Victorian townhouse which had once belonged to the Persian ambassador and there was easily enough room for everyone. Years later, Omama told my mother that the watermark on their dining room table had been made by Winston Churchill's glass when he had been the ambassador's guest before the war.

There was a long, rambling garden with stone steps leading down to a goldfish pond and a vegetable patch at the bottom where Omama let my mother and Corrado grow their own marrows. It was a happy, family house — meant for happy family memories — but my mother says she remembers feeling a sense of unease. Of course the war had cast its shadow over them, but it was more than that: Opapa was dying. He was already very ill with cancer when they arrived and would have only a few months to live.

My mother adored her grandfather and the thought of life without him was unbearable. He was a kind-hearted man who was devoted to his family. Everything he did was done with them in mind — buying Schonortli so there would be somewhere safe and fun to spend their summers; and now opening his home to them, concerned that they should still manage to be children in adult times.

Omama, who had a natural talent for raising morale, took one look at her tired, sad little grandchildren and announced cheerily: 'We'll make a cake'

The strain was clear on Omama's face and Nonna, who had always been a Daddy's girl at heart, couldn't bear to watch her father suffer. They needed then, more than ever, some diversion, anything to break the oppressive silence and give everyone a reason to smile again. Luckily, they only had to wait a few weeks — until 4 September, my mother's birthday. Omama, who had a natural talent for raising morale, took one look at her tired, sad little grandchildren and announced cheerily: 'We'll make a cake.'

No one had been expecting a birthday cake that year — even the Swiss were rationed, and money had to be saved for an uncertain future — but Omama had a secret recipe up her sleeve: Torta di Guerra. It was an ingenious creation which required very little and yet somehow still managed to taste rich and chocolatey. My mother watched as her mother and grandmother worked together, smiling at each other every now and then with heavy eyes, and when it was done they sat down together and ate, comforted by the sweetness which promised better times ahead.

OMAMA'S TORTA DI GUERRA

250 g (9 oz) yellow (polenta) flour
250 g (9 oz) plain flour
250 g (9 oz) caster sugar
250 ml (9 fl oz) full-cream milk
1 teaspoon baking powder
2 tablespoons cocoa powder
juice of 1 lemon (optional)

Preheat the oven to Gas Mark 4/180°C/fan oven 160°C.

*Mix all the ingredients well and pour into a greased and lined deep
20 cm (8-inch) cake tin.*

Bake for 30–40 minutes.

*If you have a lemon, you can squeeze the juice, mixed with a little sugar,
on top of the cake as soon as it comes out of the oven to give a sweet crust.*

Life fell into some sort of routine after that. My mother was still
too young for school, but Corrado had to go, forcing them to be
separated for the first time, and she was left to play alone in her
grandparents' big house all day. By the time he got home in the
afternoons, she was longing to hear his news, but all he wanted was
to go to his room and forget about the new children in his class
who seized every opportunity to mock him for his funny accent
and foreign ways.

Life in Italy was proving just as hard for Nonno, who was also struggling to get through each day. Milan was fast becoming too dangerous to live in – already most of the apartment blocks in their street, Via Plutarco, had been hit and some were reduced to little more than rubble. But with a growing family to provide for, he couldn't afford to leave his job. Instead, he rented accommodation in the countryside and commuted into the city each day, a treacherous and lengthy journey. Nonno grew increasingly depressed as he watched the destruction of the country he loved so much.

To console himself, he wrote letters to my mother and Corrado. They are still among the most treasured memories my mother has of him and a poignant reminder of how tender and gentle he was even at such a difficult time

To console himself, he wrote letters to my mother and Corrado. They are still among the most treasured memories my mother has of him and a poignant reminder of how tender and gentle he was even at such a difficult time. He hoped they would ensure that his children didn't forget their native language, and in each one he made up imaginative little stories about what he had been doing all day. He was fiercely patriotic and extremely proud of his heritage and, to him, it was heartbreaking to imagine his children forgetting their Italian.

His letters often included the words to traditional Italian songs and little poems he had made up. He asked his children to read and memorise them, ready to recite when they next saw him. There is one, another old Partisan song like 'Bella Ciao', called 'Aveva gli Occhi Neri', which my mother used to sing to Jem and me when we were little and which is still the best lullaby I know for calming a crying baby.

Aveva gli Occhi Neri
Aveva gli occhi neri, neri, neri
La faccia di un bambino appena nata,
L'ho visto ieri sera e l'ho baciata
L'ho visto ieri sera e l'ho baciata

La va, la va in filanda a lavorare,
Per guardagnarsi il pane col sudore
L'ho vista ieri sera a far l'amore
L'ho vista ieri sera a far l'amore.

She had eyes so black, so black, so black
And the face of a newborn baby
I saw her yesterday evening and I kissed her
I saw her yesterday evening and I kissed her

She goes to work and waits in line
To sweat and toil to earn her daily bread
I saw her yesterday evening making love
I saw her yesterday evening making love.

Festive Delight

Those letters were just one of the many things which made my mother's deep chocolate-brown eyes well with tears. So to cheer her up and give her something to pass the time, Omama decided to teach my mother and Corrado to knit.

Corrado turned up his nose at the feminine pastime at first, but he could see how enthusiastic Omama was, and in the end he reluctantly agreed to give it a go. She went into Berne and came back with a large paper bag filled with balls of coloured wool and knitting needles. That afternoon, they sat together on the veranda and she started each of them off, watching as they weaved strange and misshapen patterns, dropping stitches and getting frustrated with the long, awkward needles. They both found it tricky to get the hang of, and before long they lost interest in their new hobby. That's when she devised a little system that she knew would soon recapture their attention.

She waited until they were in bed and then, painstakingly, she unravelled each ball of wool then carefully rewound them, placing tiny brightly wrapped Lindt Napolitani chocolates here and there for the children to find. The miniature rectangles of dark chocolate – a real indulgence – came in beautiful colours, shiny lime green, red, blue, yellow, and proved the perfect antidote to a boring knitting session. The next day, when my mother and uncle started to knit, they were surprised to see these 'cioccolatini' fall out on to their laps, a sweet incentive to keep going.

I love this idea and plan to do it for my children when they are old enough. You don't have to use Napolitani, which can be tricky to get hold of. Instead, it only takes a few minutes to make a good substitute. I like the idea of tiny strips of chocolate-coated orange peel. I have included a recipe for candied orange peel, but if you like you can buy it ready made. Sicilian oranges are the best as their sharp taste complements the bitter chocolate beautifully.

DARK CHOCOLATE-COATED ORANGE PEEL – PERFECT FOR CHOCOLATE KNITTING

5 ruby oranges
450 g (1 lb) caster sugar
juice of 1 lemon
1 vanilla pod, split down the middle
    with the pulp scooped out
250 g (9 oz) dark chocolate (at least 70% cocoa solids)

First make the candied peel as this will need to soak overnight. Cut off strips of orange peel, about 4 mm ($^1/_4$ inch) thick and 2.5 cm (1 inch) long, making sure you include a thin sliver of the fruit as well. Put the slices in a saucepan, cover with water and boil for about 2 minutes, then remove and drain well. Rinse them under cold water then return them to a pan of boiling water. Repeat this process twice and then set to one side.

Place the sugar, lemon juice and vanilla pod in a deep pan and bring to the boil, stirring until all the sugar has dissolved.

Add the peel and reduce the heat. Let the mixture simmer for about 2 hours, or until the peel is soft and syrupy.

Remove the pan from the heat and place the peel and sugar syrup in a bowl to cool overnight.

The next day, remove the peel and allow it to drain.

Temper the chocolate (page 241) and leave to one side.

Butter a baking tray or sheet of baking parchment then, one at a time, dip the pieces of candied peel into the chocolate, making sure each is well coated. Place on the baking tray to drip-dry and then leave to cool. Once cooled, place in the fridge to chill until the chocolate has hardened.

You can wrap these in brightly coloured paper for a special treat or simply serve them on a small dish and eat with a thick cioccolata Fiorentina.

Makes about 35

Chocolate was beginning to give my family a sense of togetherness and, although still a rare luxury, it was slowly becoming something they turned to when spirits needed lifting. Keeping things light-hearted for the children was an almost impossible task, but Omama was determined to shield my mother and Corrado from the danger and sadness which surrounded them as far as she could and she knew that Christmas would be the perfect time to bring a little joy back into their lives.

December 1 was a happy day. My mother remembers that as a time when worries seemed to miraculously disappear and suddenly there was talk of trees and decorations and even presents – things which made her and Corrado giggle excitedly and whisper until late into the night when they were supposed to be sleeping.

The shops in Berne were transformed into magical grottoes and everywhere my mother and Corrado looked, there were gingerbread houses, chocolates to put under the tree and marzipan figures. The atmosphere in the historic city was enchanting, like the feeling you get when you open the last door on your Advent calendar and dream of Father Christmas climbing down the chimney with a sack full of presents.

The war had meant that money was scarce everywhere, even in this magical winter wonderland, but Omama and Nonna were good at making a small amount go a long way and they worked together to ensure that my mother and Corrado had a Christmas they would never forget.

The excitement began in early December when Omama dug out her secret recipes for Christmas biscuits. What little money there was, was spent on nuts, sugar, flour and eggs and soon the house was alive with sweet smells and warmed with the orangey glow from real log fires and candles. While all year round the pennies had been watched and food had been made to last, this was a chance for Omama to treat her grandchildren, and my mother skipped through the corridors singing carols to herself and feeling a million miles away from her worries about starting school and missing her father.

Omama began, early one morning, with a batch of Vanillepretzel. These delicious white vanilla biscuits were shaped to look like pretzels and letters – spelling out everyone's name. For years I wondered what it was that gave the icing such a sweet warming taste and eventually, when I was much older, my mother revealed it was a little drop of kirsch mixed in with the icing sugar as it melted.

My mother and Corrado were allowed to help make the shapes and each one made enough letters to spell out '*babbo*' (father) several times over. They struggled to fold the ends of the pretzels over properly, but it was a tricky job and they ended up with a combination of long thin ones and lots of small fat ones, which when baked looked more like shapeless blobs. It was the most fun either of them had had since they arrived and they savoured every minute of it. We always make these at Christmas now and one year I shaped them into stars and topped the icing with a few silver sugar balls.

OMAMA'S VANILLEPRETZEL

100 g (3½ oz) caster sugar
50 g (1¾ oz) vanilla sugar (page 242)
200 g (7 oz) unsalted butter, at room temperature
300 g (10½ oz) plain flour
2 egg whites
For the topping
250 g (9 oz) icing sugar
2–3 tablespoons kirsch

Cream the sugars, butter and flour together until pale and frothy, then add the unbeaten egg whites and roll into a firm ball. Cover with clingfilm and place in the refrigerator overnight.

Next day, preheat the oven to Gas Mark 3/160°C/fan oven 140°C.

Break off small chunks of the dough and shape into pretzels or letters, approximately 5 cm (2 inches) by 4 cm (1½ inches) – make sure you have enough letters to spell out everyone's name, so no one feels left out.

Bake for 10 minutes, but do not let the biscuits brown.

While they are cooking, heat the icing sugar with the kirsch and 2 tablespoons of water until dissolved.

While the biscuits are still warm, brush with the icing and place on a rack to cool. Serve with a thimble of kirsch or a big mug of creamy hot cocoa.

Makes about 40

The next batch of biscuits on the list were my mother's favourites: Spitzbuben – little round discs filled with jam and rolled in icing sugar. The children were allowed to cut the shapes with the bottoms of small liqueur glasses and fill them with the jam, always a little too much at first so that the last few only had a thin filling. These are made with the same dough as the Vanillepretzel and you can fill them with any jam you like – we used redcurrant, as they used to grow near Schonortli, but raspberry or golden plum work just as well, and sometimes Nonna used chestnut jam from a recipe which Nonno's mother had given her.

Nonna helped make a batch of Zimt Sterne, cinnamon stars, which my mother remembers as being decorative but tooth-breakingly hard, and some Honigleckerli to eat with present-opening on Christmas Eve. We don't often make either of these at home, but the one year we all spent Christmas in Schonortli they were there, and Jem and I loved the novelty of all those new sweets to enjoy.

TOOTH-BREAKING ZIMT STERNE –
CINNAMON STARS FOR HANGING ON THE TREE

3 egg whites, whisked into stiff peaks
250 g (9 oz) ground unpeeled almonds
250 g (9 oz) caster sugar
2 teaspoons cinnamon
icing sugar or chocolate icing for coating

Mix everything together to form a dough. Wrap in clingfilm and rest in the refrigerator overnight.

Next day, preheat the oven to Gas Mark 6/200°C/fan oven 180°C.

Roll the dough out thinly and cut into star shapes. Bake for 10 minutes and, while still warm, dust with icing sugar or coat with a thin chocolate icing.

Makes about 50 small stars

Jem's favourite are still Omama's little almond biscuits called Mandelmailanderli. My mother would use her special Christmas biscuit cutters to turn them into shooting stars, Christmas trees and animals when we were little. They taste best with a mug of hot cocoa, and I can remember sneaking into the dining room where my mother kept them and breaking the tails off the shooting stars, claiming later that they must have come off in the oven.

OMAMA'S MANDELMAILANDERLI

100 g (3½ oz) unsalted butter
70 g (2½ oz) caster sugar
3 egg yolks
60 g (2 oz) ground unpeeled almonds
a pinch of salt
grated zest of 1 lemon
125 g (4½ oz) plain flour

Mix the butter, sugar and two egg yolks until light and fluffy. Add the rest of the ingredients and mix well. Wrap the dough in clingfilm and rest in the refrigerator overnight.

Next day, preheat the oven to Gas Mark 4/180°C/fan oven 160°C. Roll out the dough to about 1 cm (½ inch) thick and cut into shapes. Brush with the remaining egg yolk, beaten.

Bake for 10–15 minutes.

Makes about 40

But the best, as usual, had been saved until last: Omama's Weinacht Guezi – gooey, nutty chocolate nuggets which we also called Chocolade Guezi, or simply Omama's chocolate spice biscuits. Even now, there is something magical about these little round chunks that manage to be hard and crunchy on the outside and deliciously chewy in the middle. Omama took her time over making them, and when they were ready my mother looked wide-eyed at the tray and marvelled at the cherries on top glistening in the candlelight, like tiny precious stones.

OMAMA'S WEINACHT OR CHOCOLADE GUEZI

2 medium egg whites
a few drops of vanilla essence
a pinch of cinnamon
40 g (1½ oz) dark couverture
    or good cooking chocolate, grated
30 g (1¼ oz) sweetened drinking chocolate
250 g (9 oz) caster sugar
100 g (3½ oz) ground almonds
100 g (3½ oz) ground hazelnuts
50 g (1¾ oz) vanilla sugar (page 242)
glacé cherries and whole roasted hazelnuts, to decorate

Whisk the egg whites until stiff, then beat in the vanilla essence and cinnamon.

Next fold in the grated chocolate, drinking chocolate, sugar and nuts and mix it with your hands to form a sticky dough.

Roll out the dough into long, fat sausages and coat each one in vanilla sugar. Cover with clingfilm and place in the refrigerator to harden overnight.

Next day, preheat the oven to Gas Mark 4/180°C/fan oven 160°C.

Cut the dough into slices, about 1 cm (½ inch) thick, and place half a glacé cherry or a roasted hazelnut on top of each.

Bake for 10 minutes – the biscuits should still be soft when you take them out of the oven.

Place on a cooling rack and eat when cool.

Makes about 60

It was the worst kind of torture, knowing that all those biscuits were waiting temptingly in the dining room for Christmas Eve. But luckily St Nicholas's Day was just around the corner and my mother and Corrado knew that meant they would have something sweet to tide them over. Tucked up in their little wooden beds on the night of 5 December, waiting for some much-needed Christmas make-believe, they listened as Nonna told them the story of the kindly old priest who once left gifts for good little girls and boys, and who now travels through the starry night sky on 5 December, delivering tiny parcels of chocolate and oranges, which he hides in the slippers that children have left for him outside their bedroom doors.

Jem and I were brought up on the tradition too, and my mother used to fill our slippers with chocolates wrapped in coloured paper and amber-skinned nectarines that we regarded somewhat suspiciously as taking up far too much room.

My mother didn't dare think such greedy thoughts when she was a girl and she and Corrado were always grateful for anything Omama gave them. That year, they found a Cailler praline bar each and St Nicholas also left them a bar of their favourite chocolate. My mother's was Rayon, which was a little like Italian torrone. It was made from honey and praline blended with milk chocolate and came in a bright orange wrapper.

I have devised my own version of this. It's the perfect 'slipper chocolate' and is good enough to give away as Christmas gifts. The beauty of this sweet is in the presentation, which is so simple and yet gratifyingly effective.

Bitter Chocolate 'Rayon' Nuggets

250 g (9 oz) clear honey
2 egg whites
250 g (9 oz) caster sugar
450 g (1 lb) blanched almonds
225 g (8 oz) hazelnuts
2 teaspoons diced candied orange peel
1 teaspoon grated lemon zest
2 teaspoons zucca (candied pumpkin)
To decorate
600 g (1 lb 5 oz) bitter dark chocolate
    (at least 70% cocoa solids)
1 tablespoon unsalted butter
a few slivers of blanched almonds
a handful of pistachio nuts
crystallised violet petals
3 pieces of candied orange peel, thinly sliced

Heat the honey in a heavy-bottomed pan for 5 minutes. Beat the egg whites until stiff and fold them into the honey.

In a separate pan, mix the sugar and 2 tablespoons of water and bring to the boil without stirring. It should turn a caramel colour. Add to the honey mixture and leave to cool until it starts to thicken.

Add the remaining ingredients.

Lay down a sheet of rice paper and pour the mixture on top. Leave it to cool for about 20 minutes.

When it has set, cut the torrone into small, thick rectangular bars, about 4 cm (1½ inches) long, smoothing them as much as possible with a palette knife.

Temper the chocolate (page 241) and stir in the butter before pouring it over the top of each one to coat well. Before the chocolate has completely set, decorate each bar with a few slivers of blanched almonds, a thin slice of candied orange peel, some chopped pistachios and a couple of crystallised violet petals. Leave to cool in the fridge.

Makes about 40

They celebrated Christmas the Italian way that year – eating a meal of tortellini in brodo and fish on Christmas Eve and singing Italian songs before opening their presents in the evening. Omama had bought a huge Christmas tree, which she put at the foot of the stairs in the entranceway and decorated with oranges, Zimt Sterne and Lindt Napolitani. It was a breathtaking sight, towering over them with its shimmering baubles and tempting little cioccolatini like a friendly giant, and beneath it there were enticing-looking presents wrapped in colourful boxes.

My mother remembers getting her first doll and thinking she was the most beautiful thing she had ever seen. She had long blonde tresses and a lovely pink dress and my mother spent the rest of the night combing and plaiting her hair, wishing hers was like that. Several weeks later, Corrado – who was fast discovering how little it took to reduce his sister to tears – crept up on her as she played and grabbed the precious doll. He ran to the kitchen with it where he took a pair of scissors from the drawer and cut off the beautiful, long blonde plaits. When my mother saw what had happened, she cried and cried and ran to Omama, who promised to take it to the doll's 'hairdressers' in Berne. My mother waited eagerly by the door for her to return, but to her dismay the hairdresser had given the doll a rather dull brown perm. She played with it a few times to show willing, but it was never quite the same after that, and she learnt never to trust older brothers again.

On Christmas Day itself, Omama and Opapa made the best of the provisions they had, roasting a chicken with some of the marrows and other vegetables from their garden. For dessert, Omama made another version of Torta Di Guerra with some raisins and a tin of condensed milk – the fake white chocolate she used to send my mother and Corrado in her food parcels. They ate it with spiced oranges and a dish of Christmas biscuits and all felt, for a few hours at least, like whole people again.

SPECIAL CHRISTMAS TORTA DI GUERRA – OR OMAMA'S WHITE CHOCOLATE CAKE FOR THOSE WHO KNOW …

380-g can of condensed milk
grated zest of 1 lemon
50 g (1¾ oz) raisins, sultanas or pine nuts, depending on
what you have in your store cupboard
200 g (7 oz) plain flour
1 teaspoon baking powder
2 small eggs, separated

Preheat the oven to Gas Mark 4/180°C/fan oven 160°C.

Combine all the ingredients apart from the egg whites.

Whisk the egg whites into stiff peaks and fold them into the mixture.

*Spoon the mixture into a greased and lined deep 20-cm (8-inch) cake tin
and bake for 35–40 minutes.*

Time crept on slowly for my mother after that, and each day Italy's
fate seemed more and more uncertain. Mussolini, the leader who
had once promised his people an efficient infrastructure, a healthy
economy and plenty of jobs, was now seen more and more as an
unwelcome puppet to the Nazis, far more interested in his own
political gain than the welfare of his people.

Despite being surrounded by her closest family, my mother
remembers feeling strangely alone at that time. In those months
after Christmas there was little to make her feel like a child.
Nonna had her mind on the baby growing inside her and her
husband so far away, and Omama was preoccupied with Opapa,
who was by then desperately ill. It was then that chocolate became
her greatest ally – her Christmas memories gave her a warm,
comforting glow and reminded her that she would always have her
family around her, no matter what. As Easter approached, she
found herself getting excited again, smiling as she thought about
the surprises Omama would have in store for her and Corrado.

In Italy, Pasqua is a huge celebration. Traditionally, it is a
holiday when families spend time together, preparing tasty post-
fast meals, sweet breads and desserts to enjoy after church. The

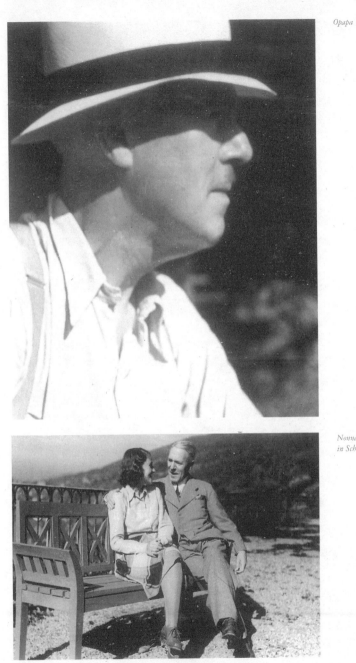

Nonna with Opapa
in Schonortli

shops are filled with panettones and the more traditional Easter Colomba and trays of sweets and chocolates. My mother used to look lovingly at the chocolate eggs, with '*Buona Pasqua*' written on the side in white icing. They were huge confections, wrapped in shiny papers and topped with flowers and a bow. She did eventually get one – when she was a little older – but she admits now that the Swiss ones always tasted better.

My mother pined for the Easter delicacies she had enjoyed with her family while they were still living in Italy but, little did she know, she was in for an even bigger treat in Switzerland. In the shop windows, the Hansel and Gretel houses, marzipan fruit baskets and chocolate biscuits from Christmas had been replaced with marzipan bunnies with chocolate eyes, chocolate truffle eggs wrapped in gold paper, and larger eggs, nestled tantalisingly between sugar mice and candied fruit. There was one type of egg all the children wanted, smaller than the Italian ones but made with creamy milk chocolate and decorated with sugared almonds, and my mother secretly hoped she would get one.

Omama's beautiful, slightly overgrown garden was perfect for Easter egg hunts and she taught my mother and Corrado how to make their own chocolate eggs. First she showed them how to make a bain-marie and melt the chocolate, then she helped them pour it into her special moulds which gave the finished eggs a cracked effect – just like the ones in the shops. Making eggs is almost as much fun as eating them and the best part is that you can add just about anything you like, provided you have some suitably shiny paper and a length of ribbon to wrap them with. The ones Omama made were just plain milk chocolate but you can add hazelnuts and raisins too for a chunkier texture or orange rind and Cointreau for a romantic gift.

My mother with her
Easter eggs in Berne

Easter egg hunt, Berne

OMAMA'S EASTER EGGS –
FOR HIDING IN VEGETABLE PATCHES

You will need an egg mould for this, some shiny wrapping paper and plenty of ribbon.

200 g (7 oz) fine milk chocolate
50 g (1³/₄ oz) chopped hazelnuts (optional)
50 g (1³/₄ oz) raisins, soaked in rum (optional)
a little caster sugar

Melt and temper the chocolate (page 241) until it has a glossy sheen. Add the nuts and raisins, if using, then pour into the mould and swirl around until the whole half egg is coated. Repeat with as many moulds as you can until all the chocolate is used up. Place in the refrigerator to set.

When the chocolate has set, push the eggs out of the moulds and place on a sheet of greaseproof paper.

Melt some caster sugar in a pan until it has dissolved to form a caramel, then brush some around the edge of one egg half with a confectioner's brush and quickly set the other half of the egg on top before it hardens. Repeat with all the eggs.

Wrap the eggs in paper and tie with a ribbon.

Makes two 5-cm (2-inch) eggs

For weeks, Nonna and Omama spoke in conspiratorial whispers every time the children were near and disappeared on 'secret' trips to Berne, returning with mysterious parcels. All this coming and going added to my mother's excitement and when Easter finally arrived, she awoke early and full of beans. Nonna and Omama spent the morning in the garden, hiding handfuls of tiny praline eggs, wrapped in green paper, and some larger milk chocolate eggs that they had made. My mother wore a pretty white skirt and cardigan and had a pink ribbon in her hair. She and Corrado took their time over the hunt, both eager to be the one to find the first egg. They were allowed a little wicker basket each and when they had found all the eggs, they laid them out on the garden table for counting. Once they had finished sharing them, Omama brought out a very special surprise – one of those delicious nutty eggs they had seen in the shops.

Opapa survived just long enough to see his little granddaughter and hold her in his arms, and when he died everyone looked to Rosalba to fill the hole in their hearts – a heavy burden for such tiny shoulders

Years later, my parents would lavish chocolates and Easter eggs on Jem and me, far too many to eat, enjoying the luxury of being able to spoil us. But for my mother, nothing will ever come close to those creamy Alpine eggs on Easter day in her grandparents' house.

By the time Easter was over, Nonna was already heavily pregnant and, two months later, Rosalba was born. Nonno was desperately sad to have missed the birth of his third child and begged Nonna to describe her to him in minute detail in her letters. Opapa survived just long enough to see his little granddaughter and hold her in his arms, and when he died everyone looked to Rosalba to fill the hole in their hearts – a heavy burden for such tiny shoulders.

It wasn't until her baptism, four months later, that Nonno could get special dispensation to go and visit his family. It was an emotional reunion – the strain clearly showing on Nonno's thin, tired face, while Nonna was still mourning the death of her father. But he was determined to make the most of his freedom and spent every second of it holding his beautiful new daughter.

Leaving, for him, was even worse then than the first time all those months ago in the mountains, but my mother remembers seeing him again not long after that. She was allowed to visit him at the border, with Nonna, but they had to talk to him through a wire mesh and she couldn't help feeling that it was like visiting a caged animal. Yet somehow there was a feeling of hope in the air – as though, for the first time, they knew this separation was not going to last for ever. Within the year they would all be back in Milan, a family again at last.

Nonna and Nonno with little Rosalba

Mussolini had sealed his country's fate the day he shook hands with Hitler, and the Italians hated him for it. This time, the Partisans weren't taking any chances and, along with his mistress Carla Petacci, he was executed by firing squad on 29 April 1945. His body was hung by its feet outside an Esso gas station in Piazzale Loreto in Milan – a clear sign that his rule was finally over. It was the best thing that had happened to the country for a long time, but for my mother it was just another reminder that life would never again be innocent and carefree. She and Corrado passed the hook from which he had dangled, in the tram on their way to school each morning and even though they turned their heads at the last minute, they were still haunted by the picture of what he must have looked like.

There was less time now for 'La Titi', as my mother was affectionately known, and she couldn't help feeling sorry for herself.

Life in Switzerland would soon seem like a strange and distant dream and my mother sensed that things would never be the same again. In the space of a year Opapa had died, leaving the house in Berne emptier than it had ever been, and Rosalba had arrived. There was less time now for 'La Titi', as my mother was affectionately known, and she couldn't help feeling sorry for herself. To make matters worse, she hated school – she hadn't spoken more than a few words of Italian for the best part of two years and was struggling to keep up.

The war had put a huge strain on the country's resources and most schools had been closed down due to damage or lack of funds. My mother's consisted of one large classroom where everyone did their lessons together and Corrado, once her greatest ally, was now at that age where having a little sister tagging along behind him would have seriously compromised his image. He told her she wasn't allowed to sit next to him in class and warned her off his friends, forcing her further into her own, private little world. It was a lonely time and my mother – now a serious girl with her curly dark hair tied back in neat plaits – longed to escape.

In the end, it was Opapa who gave her a way out. Fortunately he had had the foresight to invest his money wisely during the war – in Schonortli – and now there was at least somewhere where my

mother and her family could go to get away from the oppressive heat of Milan and the drudgery of everyday life. So, whenever Nonno could get the time off work, they packed their bags and headed for the quiet security of Switzerland, where my mother was allowed to be a child again.

Nonna taught her to swim in the little pool at the bottom of the garden and she picked berries with Corrado and her cousins in the evenings, when the crickets were out and there was a cool soothing breeze in the air. She was allowed to speak German again and enjoyed the fuss and attention she got from Frau Kempf and her husband who lived next door and Herr Bigler down the road, who kept chickens and let my mother take fresh eggs home for dinner. It seemed like heaven to her and brought all the memories of Opapa and better times flooding back. She sat at the old piano in the *Spielzimmer* and practised her Chopin, thinking of her beloved grandfather and wondering if he knew how happy she was there.

My mother remembers her lying flat out on the floor of their apartment one stifling day in August, hoping the cold tiles would cool her down

Schonortli was a comfort to everyone, and Omama, who needed cheering as much as her little grandchildren, would greet them at the big oak door, a broad smile on her handsome face, opening her hands to reveal a bar of Rayon and a stick of praline for my mother and Corrado to share. My mother would suck each mouthful slowly, hoping the taste would stay on her tongue for ever.

Over the years, Schonortli would provide my mother with the perfect antidote to life in Milan. Nonna felt it too – she grew to love Italy, but she never got used to the summer heat. My mother remembers her lying flat out on the floor of their apartment one stifling day in August, hoping the cold tiles would cool her down. She missed the icy lakes of home, the warm dry sun, and the thunderstorms which erupted over the mountains in late summer, breaking the dark sky and bringing cool fresh raindrops the size of pebbles.

Omama knew her grandchildren didn't see much of their Italian grandparents, so she tried her best to make up for it when they came to visit her, treating them to all the things they couldn't have at home. Despite being a strong woman – a true survivor – Omama hated living alone and she looked forward more than anything to having someone with whom to go to her favourite tearooms. She was a modest woman who disapproved of excess, always telling my mother and Corrado to leave room for a slice of bread and butter after dinner to avoid overeating, but cakes were her downfall and she found every possible excuse to indulge her sweet tooth.

One summer in Schonortli, my mother seemed unusually quiet. There had been a fourth addition to the family – Corrina – and although she was a little clown who brought a smile to everyone's face, her arrival meant that Nonna now had even less time to spend with my mother. My mother would sit in the *salotto* all day, her nose in a book, shaking her head when Rosalba asked her to come and play and only picking at her lunch. Omama hated seeing her like that and decided it was time for some chocolate therapy. So she chose an elegant patisserie in Berne called Tschirren and invited my mother out to tea. The shop window was mesmerising, like something straight out of a fairy tale, with replicas of the sights of Berne – the fountain in the heart of the city, the cathedral, the canton's bear mascots – all made of chocolate. Inside there was a huge selection of cakes and my mother, who was already feeling decidedly happier, ordered a hot chocolate and a Japonais – a small mille-feuille of meringue and light chocolate mousse, covered in more chocolate mousse and decorated with chopped nuts and a tiny pink chocolate button. It was delicious, crunchy on the outside and sweet and chewy on the inside, and she took her time eating it.

Omama gave her the best advice she knew that day, telling her that if she followed what was in her heart, she would end up on the right path. My mother decided that if Omama could survive losing her husband, she too could cope with a little change and vowed to be braver, letting the power of chocolate and her grandmother's kind words slowly wash over her. One year, when she was much older, she was in Switzerland for her birthday and Nonna ordered a giant Japonais for a special treat from a cake shop in Oberhofen – it was the only year they didn't have Napoleon's Torte, but somehow nobody minded. I have also eaten this cake with Nonna and Nonno in Lugano and was surprised to find how simple it is to make, especially if you use Omama's Chocolate Mousse recipe for the filling.

> *My mother decided that if Omama could survive losing her husband, she too could cope with a little change and vowed to be braver, letting the power of chocolate and her grandmother's kind words slowly wash over her*

JAPONAIS – CHOCOLATE THERAPY

    4 egg whites
    250 g (9 oz) caster sugar
    2 quantities of Omama's Chocolate Mousse (page 115)
    150 g (5½ oz) flaked almonds
    3 pink Smarties

Preheat the oven to Gas Mark ½/120°C/fan oven 100°C.

Whisk the egg whites until stiff then slowly add the sugar, whisking until it has all been incorporated.

Divide the meringue mix between two 23-cm (9-inch) square cake tins and bake for about 50 minutes, or until firm.

While the meringues are cooling, make Omama's mousse.

Spread a thick layer of mousse on one of the meringues and sandwich the other one on top. Cover the whole cake in mousse and decorate with the flaked almonds. Cut the cake lengthways in three, to make three smaller cakes and place a Smartie on top of each.

Eat with a smile and some good grandmotherly advice.

Makes 3 cakes

Omama loved taking my mother and Corrado into Berne, happy to show them the sights and teach them the history of the city where she and their mother were born. She told them that there used to be an onion market in the old quarter each week, known as the Zibele Markt, where stallholders sold their vegetables under the huge mechanical cuckoo clock. The market no longer existed when my mother was a girl, but had been replaced by a custom which still goes on today – of selling baskets of marzipan vegetables to passers by. Omama sometimes treated the children to one, which they took an age to eat. One time she bought Rosalba and Corrina a long marzipan carrot each. Corrina, a patient, frugal little girl, kept hers on the window ledge in their room back in Milan, looking at it every now and then but never taking a bite. Rosalba, who was feisty and impatient, ate hers in a hurry and then devised a little plan to get Corrina's: by eating away at it from the back. She did this every night for weeks, taking a tiny bite each time, until it was so hollow it couldn't stand up on its own and fell tellingly on to the floor below. Corrina didn't speak to Rosalba for days, but it taught her a valuable lesson and she always ate her sweets quickly after that.

Even walks were punctuated with chocolate treats on those wonderful holidays, and Nonna would always stop at the little milk bar in Oberhofen after a day in the mountains and buy a Black Forest gateau for everyone to share back at Schonortli. This was quite different from the travesty that is best avoided on some menus these days. It was unfathomably soft and airy and the chocolate cream filling was rich and slightly bitter. Cream in Switzerland is virtually a dessert in itself; the whole cake was covered in it and made for a welcome treat after a hard day's exercise.

It wasn't just during the day that chocolate played an important part in the children's lives. My mother remembers a special midnight ritual initiated by Corrado which became a tradition that got passed down to my cousins and me too. There was always plenty of cream and butter in the fridge, fresh from Frau Kempf's farm just up the road, and Omama kept a bar or two of chocolate in the kitchen cupboards for emergencies – perfect midnight feast material. One year Corrado and my mother's cousin Hildi crept downstairs once everyone else was in bed and decided to make some fudge. When they had found everything they needed, they went to get the others. The older ones showed the youngsters what to do and my mother was allowed to mix the sugary concoction with a wooden spoon until it hardened enough to be put in the tray and scored. There was an extravagant amount of childish whispering and excitement as they all dug their spoons in, eating it with the nervous hunger which came from knowing they could be found out at any moment. The fudge never usually lasted until morning, but one time they left the tray in the sink, unwashed, and the cook told Nonna, who made sure after that that the kitchen door was always firmly closed and that the children were safely tucked up in bed as they should be.

NIDELTAFELI – MIDNIGHT-FEAST FUDGE

500 ml (18 fl oz) full-cream milk or cream
750 g (1 lb 10 oz) caster sugar
50 g (1³/₄ oz) dark chocolate

Put all the ingredients in a heavy-bottomed pan and melt over a low heat for about 30 minutes, stirring all the time. When all the ingredients have dissolved, pour into a rectangular baking tray, about 18 x 28 cm (7 x 11 inches), and place in the refrigerator to cool.

Score into small squares and eat quietly.

My mother (second from front) at her First Holy Communion

My mother with Nonno and Corrado at her First Holy Communion

Years later, when I was a little girl, my cousins encouraged me to help them make Nonna's Napoleon's Torte late at night. We had such fun whispering and running to the stairs to see if anyone was coming, but my mother – who knew exactly what we were up to – still insists her fudge was better.

Omama had become my mother's greatest confidante over the years and she always turned to her when she needed advice on school work or friendships, cherishing her unerringly good advice, so when the time came for her to make her First Holy Communion, she begged Nonna to invite Omama to watch. Her First Communion was as important to my mother as my father's bar mitzvah was to him when he was a boy. She practised the ceremony for months, along with her best friend, Lele, and it was agreed that they would hold hands in the procession. The rules were clear: dresses must be simple and respectable, no fuss or extras, and hair had to be tied neatly back off the face. Nonna followed the instructions to the letter, but when the day came, my mother was mortified to find that Lele was wearing an elaborate gown with more frills and trimmings than a Christmas turkey, her blonde hair flowing prettily over her shoulders.

> *The rules were clear: dresses must be simple and respectable, no fuss or extras, and hair had to be tied neatly back off the face*

But nothing could spoil that day for my mother, who felt a deep sense of pride at being able to share such a special occasion with the people she loved most. After the ceremony, Omama treated her to a delicious creamy hot chocolate at a chic little patisserie in the heart of Milan called Vanini. It was there that she gave her her *madonina* – a delicate gold chain with a Madonna pendant, which she still treasures to this day.

Vanini was an intimate little eatery, a place where Nonna would sometimes go to for biscuits and fruit tarts if she was having friends round. But her favourite patisserie was Sant Ambreus, which boasted the best Gateau St-Honoré in the city – a decadent creation made with layers of sponge and chocolate cream and covered in profiteroles.

St-Honoré is one of those desserts you would only make for weddings, christenings and very special occasions, but it is the most glorious piece of confection you will ever eat. I can't pretend I have ever made it myself, but two cocoa sponges, one quantity of Omama's Chocolate Mousse and a few shop-bought profiteroles ought to make a pretty good imitation.

For a while, holidays in Schonortli kept everyone sane, but eventually life picked up in Milan too and some sort of order returned. Nonno was climbing quickly through the ranks at work, and even school was beginning to seem less daunting – at last the family seemed to have turned a corner and the effects of the war years began to fade.

Zio Enrico and Zia Marcella were always asking after the children, but my mother hardly saw them and longed to spend more time getting to know her father's side of the family – her Italian roots. So on the rare occasions she saw her Italian nonna and nonno, she was determined to enjoy every second. Her nonna was small and a little hunched and reminded my mother of a favourite dress that needed ironing. She remembers her giving them home-baked biscotti and laughing when Corrado said '*bitte, bitte*' (please, please) in his cute German accent.

Nonna Argia was an excellent cook and loved spoiling them all with good food when they were there, but the thing my mother remembers most was her Crema di Castagne – chestnut jam. She made it with vanilla and sugar and turned it into vermicelli or spread it thickly on slices of *pane rustica*. The children loved it and it had the advantage of being at least halfway healthy. Nonna was so impressed she asked for the recipe, and wrote it down in her trusty cookery book, which already contained all of Omama's recipes. Making chestnut jam is time consuming and fiddly but extremely rewarding, and it is the perfect accompaniment to good dark chocolate. I make it in winter and have spread a thin layer of it at the bottom of a creamy chocolate tart for a pre-Christmas party or on Omama's Spitzbuben instead of raspberry jam, but it works just as well with apple Kuchen in summer or mixed with cream for a roulade filling.

> *St-Honoré is one of those desserts you would only make for very special occasions, but it is the most glorious piece of confection you will ever eat*

NONNA ARGIA'S CREMA DI CASTAGNE

1.8 kg (4 lb) unshelled chestnuts
750 g (1 lb 10 oz) caster sugar
1 vanilla pod, split lengthways
a pinch of cinnamon (optional)

Preheat the oven to Gas Mark 6/200°C/fan oven 180°C.

*Cut a cross in the top of each chestnut and roast in the oven for
45 minutes, or until soft. Leave them to cool completely then remove
the shells.*

*Put the sugar, vanilla pod and cinnamon, if using, in a heavy-bottomed
pan with about 125 ml (4 fl oz) water and heat to dissolve the sugar.
Bring to the boil, then reduce to a simmer and add the chestnuts. Cook
for about 15–20 minutes. Remove the vanilla pod and pass the mixture
through a blender until smooth.*

*Store for up to 2 months in sterilised containers, topped with wax paper
circles, and eat with friends and good chocolate. Refrigerate once opened.*

Makes 900 g (2 lb)

Nonno adored his parents and would have loved his children to have the same relationship with them that they had with Omama. But there never seemed to be enough time to see everyone and by the time they died, my mother realised, sadly, that she had hardly known them. That's why the recipes mean so much. Even now, the smell of roasting chestnuts reminds her of her nonna and every time she makes risotto Milanese or chocolate biscotti and zabaglione – all those wonderful traditional dishes her nonna used to make so well – she thinks of her and dreams of Italy.

Those years were so many things to my mother; she battled with a painful shyness she puts down to having to change schools so often, and she felt in constant competition for Nonna's affection. But there was a sense of togetherness too, the warm feeling she got in the pit of her stomach when she lay awake at night listening to the gentle breathing of her sisters, knowing she would never be alone in the world. She admired her mother for the strength and courage she had shown during the war and her father, who worked so hard to provide her with the schooling, piano lessons and ski classes she loved – all the things he had never had as a child. Those were the years that made her the person she is today, but when she wanted an escape, it was always to Switzerland that she turned.

For Omama, a healthy walk always ended with a rather more unhealthy trip to one of her favourite patisseries, and birthdays were an elaborate excuse for yet more dressed-up, fancy-looking chocolate. One year on my mother's birthday, she ordered a cake from a patisserie in Berne with a chocolate icing replica of the cathedral in Oberhofen on top as decoration. My mother remembers looking at in stunned silence, wondering how long she could make it last. Of course it was gone in no time, but the memory still lingers on her tongue like a sweet souvenir.

My mother loved Switzerland as a child and felt a strong affinity with the country which had harboured her in such dark times. In Milan, Nonna insisted she attend a Swiss-speaking school which meant doing all her lessons in German and, although it was hard at the time, she says now that it gave her a greater understanding of where she came from. The school often organised skiing trips in winter and one year my mother was allowed to go with them to Davos in the south-east of Switzerland, near St Moritz. She was 13, a fit, sporty teenager and already a very competent skier, having had plenty of practice with her cousins in Schonortli.

It was the Christmas holidays and the group was staying in a large hall of residence near the Parsen mountain. In the mornings they were herded off to the *Kinderheim* (ski school), but the afternoons were their own to explore and she loved it. The freedom of the slopes and all that fresh white snow had made her feel that she could breathe again, and she was determined to enjoy every second. She had already made a few good friends and, one afternoon, she and some of the other girls in her class walked to the nearby village and went into one of the little cake shops which lined the streets. They each had a bit of pocket money, not quite enough for a drink and a cake, but they could afford one of the local Parsenstein – huge chocolate truffles about the size of a tennis ball, with milk chocolate on the inside and a dark coating. The name means 'rocks from the Parsen mountain' and they were the most shamelessly indulgent thing my mother had ever seen. She carried hers back to her room and vowed to take only tiny bites of it at a time, savouring the rich creamy taste. These are the simplest, quickest things to make and a great post-snowball fight pick-me-up for cold children.

COLD-WEATHER PARSENSTEIN

150 ml (5 fl oz) double cream
1 vanilla pod, split lengthways
450 g (1 lb) milk chocolate couverture
about 25 g (1 oz) unsalted butter
50 g (1½ oz) mixed nuts, roughly chopped

For the coating
150 g (5½ oz) dark chocolate (don't worry too much
    about the quality and cocoa content)
chocolate sprinkles
1 tablespoon rum (optional)

Place the cream in a heavy-bottomed pan with the vanilla pod and simmer for 3–5 minutes. Remove from the heat and leave for 30 minutes to infuse.

Meanwhile, chop the milk chocolate and butter and place in a mixing bowl with the nuts.

When you are ready to make the truffles, remove the vanilla pod from the cream, return the pan to a high heat and bring to the boil. Pour the cream straight on to the chocolate, and stir until you have a thick creamy ganache.

Leave the mixture to cool then use a big spoon to scoop out enough to make a ball about the size of the palm of your hand. Roll into rough shapes and leave on a sheet of baking parchment.

Melt the dark chocolate. Dip the balls into the melted chocolate then roll them straightaway in the sprinkles. Leave them to set in the refrigerator.

Eat with a tall glass of fresh milk. You can add the rum to the coating chocolate if it's particularly cold outside and the children are in bed.

Makes about 6

The ski trip was such a success that the following year Nonna enrolled my mother and Corrado in a ski school in Murren, not too far from Schonortli. They stayed in the *Kinderheim* for a few nights and although my mother was not yet 15, she and Corrado were both allowed a glass of Glühwein on New Year's Eve, which they drank with a traditional cheese fondue. Instead of forfeits, they played the lead game. Each person is given a few pieces of lead and a little booklet and the idea is to melt the lead nuggets over the fondue flame and drop them in a bowl of icy water. Depending on what shape they formed, the booklet gave predictions for the coming year. It was great fun and my mother learnt that she would come into a huge sum of money, meet the man of her dreams and find a successful job – not bad for a 14-year-old schoolgirl.

The next day was the last day of ski school and the organisers had arranged a slalom competition. Corrado entered, while my mother stood at the finish line with a stopwatch and a little blue and white flag. She watched eagerly as they all came down, cheering her friends and looking out keenly for her brother. She waited and waited, but there was no sign of him. Her heart thumping, she ran from her post to alert someone that Corrado was lost. He was a very good skier, so to take so long was ominous. He was eventually found halfway down the course, doubled over in agony, his leg broken. After the initial shock, Corrado quite enjoyed the drama of it all and let his new friends sign his plaster cast, repeating the story to anyone who would listen, making the slope icier and the pain greater each time.

Fortunately, Corrado's accident hadn't put my mother off the slopes and she begged Nonna and Nonno to let her go back to Switzerland soon. She loved the thrill of trying out new runs and had always dreamed of skiing over one of the glaciers. But her parents could never have afforded to send her on a trip like that so instead, the following summer, she found herself some work experience with the tourist board in Murren. The job itself was unchallenging and my mother had little in common with her much older colleagues. But there was one huge attraction: her employer agreed to pay her with a trip to Bernina, walking over the glaciers with a guide.

The experience far exceeded her high expectations. The peaks were sun-kissed and dazzling, shimmering like an ocean of morning dew, and the views down to the valley were mesmerising.

They stayed one night in a wooden hut and ate mountain risotto, prepared by the guide on his little travel stove, and drank hot chocolate brews to warm her enough to sleep. In the morning, after a few hours walking, the guide told her to sit on her snow pick and slide down the piste, following him on a safe path. Nonna, a careful, responsible skier, would have been horrified if she knew what my mother had been allowed to do, but it was the best fun she had ever had – exhilarating, dangerous and far more character-building than sitting in a dull office.

Once you fall in love with the mountains, they stay with you for ever and my mother found herself returning to them whenever she could. When she was 18, she spent a year in Berne, living with Omama for part of her stay and her aunt Hildi for the rest of the time, and working for a film company during the day.

Nonna hoped the year would encourage my mother to develop her language skills – she already spoke French, English and German fluently. But her eldest daughter's job prospects weren't the only thing on Nonna's mind. My mother was now the same age she had been when she met Nonno, and Nonna decided that the time had come to groom her for married life.

My mother was now the same age she had been when she met Nonno, and Nonna decided that the time had come to groom her for married life

By the time my mother returned to Milan, Nonna had already enrolled her in a cookery class, just as Omama had done for her. She was extremely excited to have found a course which was run by the chef who used to cook for the King of Italy and, aware of the power of traditional Milanese snobbery, she thought it would ensure my mother would impress any future mother-in-law.

He proved an excellent teacher and my mother soon discovered she had a natural talent for cooking, copying down his recipes in a plain notebook she had bought herself, just as Nonna and Omama had done before her. He started with the basics: showing his young protégés how to make every type of pastry from choux to shortcrust, sauces, stocks, pasta and simple main meals. But his forte was cakes, and in the last few lessons he showed them how to make his signature dishes: crème caramel with raspberry coulis; crème brûlée with lemon and dark chocolate; chocolate and

Anita Risito

LE
MIE
RICETTE

PEI

My mother's recipe book, front cover

hazelnut Torte with vermicelli – a dazzling array of desserts which would be sure to please any husband to be. She tried them all out on Nonna and Nonno, finding that she too, like her mother and grandmother before her, loved the soothing therapy of sweet cooking; and the lessons must have stuck because I have never once seen her make a flat sponge or a heavy soufflé.

Yet despite this, life in Milan did not prove as fulfilling as my mother had hoped. Rosalba and Corrina were still little girls and she was itching to leave home and find some independence. She had discovered that she had a flair for drawing, and her ambition was to become a fashion designer. She loved clothes, even though she had little money to spend on them, and she occupied all her spare time sketching dresses she had seen in magazines, and creating ballgowns and beautifully tailored suits.

Nonna and Nonno were disappointed. They had wanted her to have a respectable nine-to-five job with good prospects, but they could see her enthusiasm, and eventually they gave in and allowed her to attend fashion college in Milan. She passed all her classes with top grades and won a place to work as an assistant with one of the most famous contemporary designers working in Milan at the time, Marucelli. She was already in her fifties by the time my mother met her – a real character, with her grey hair tied into an incongruous bun that sat on top of her head, and a collection of colourful kaftans that she wore every day. She was a bit like the Vivienne Westwood of her day, creating elaborate, hugely creative clothes which no one could ever imagine wearing but loved to look at none the less. My mother was one of a group of girls working for her, all of them design assistants who were prepared to work ridiculous hours and do any job to make sure the collections were the best they could be. One summer, they were putting on an important show in Florence and my mother remembers sitting in the train from Milan, sewing the hems on chiffon gowns, desperately trying to hide them from a rival company sitting in the same carriage.

The Florentine show was being hosted by Count Chigi, and on the last day of this elaborate annual event he organised a huge ball at the Palazzo Belvedere. The setting was stunningly beautiful, with frescoed walls, rustic wooden tables laid with white cloths, and little tealight candles lighting the paths in the rambling grounds. There was a feast with a medieval theme, and Marucelli had told her girls to dress in costume, giving them enough material to make their own dresses. My mother and her friends spent hours making the headdresses and tight corsets, but when they arrived they were embarrassed to find that they were the only ones in fancy dress.

The setting was stunningly beautiful, with frescoed walls, rustic wooden tables laid with white cloths, and little tealight candles

It didn't spoil the party, however, and all the girls enjoyed the best views of Florence, sipping champagne cocktails and staring as dishes of whole roast piglet and plates of zuccotto were brought past. Zuccotto is a traditional Florentine dessert, a bit like a bombe, made with trifle sponges and filled with either cream or ice cream. It is dome shaped and looks rather like a pumpkin – hence its name – and is decorated with stripes of cocoa powder and icing sugar. That night, it was made with cream and zucca and had a rich chocolate centre. My mother was so taken with it she has been making it ever since for dinner parties, and she taught me how to make it when I was very little. It's the most diet-mocking dessert imaginable, pure, unadulterated calories, but the best kind of comfort food and very simple to put together – which makes it an ideal cake to prepare with children. We always use dark chocolate for the filling together with tiny cubes of candied melon, angelica and pumpkin, which give it a nice bite.

ZUCCOTTO

1 packet of trifle sponges
amaretto for soaking the sponges
200 ml (7 fl oz) double cream
50 g (1³/₄ oz) zucca (candied-pumpkin), chopped
50 g (1³/₄ oz) angelica, chopped
100 g (3¹/₂ oz) dark chocolate chips
cocoa powder and icing sugar for the topping

Soak the trifle sponges in amaretto and leave for a while to infuse.

Line a pudding basin with foil. Press in the soaked sponge to line the basin and leave in the refrigerator to cool.

Whip the cream until stiff, then add the candied fruits together with a little icing sugar. Fill the pudding basin with the cream, reserving about 4 tablespoons.

Melt the chocolate in a bain-marie. Let cool, then mix with the reserved cream. Make a hole in the centre of the pudding and pour the chocolate mixture in. Leave it in the refrigerator to set.

When you are nearly ready to serve, turn the pudding on to a plate and remove the foil. Sift alternate stripes of cocoa powder and icing sugar on top. The easiest way to do this is to make a template from greaseproof paper so that when it is placed on top of the cake the paper edges will keep the cocoa and icing sugar separate.

Eat with care and a cup of cioccolata Fiorentina.

Serves 8–10

That year with Marucelli taught my mother a lot about the fashion world. She had intended to stay and learn as much from the designer as she could, but a difficult relationship was making her miserable in Milan and Nonna – ever hopeful that she might come to her senses and return to her languages – suggested that she go and live in London for a few months to get over her broken heart. She had hoped a few months would be all it took to bring a smile back to my mother's face. It worked, and nearly 40 years on that smile is still there.

CHAPTER 6:

London Calling

*L*ove, like good chocolate, can not be ignored, and when it hits you it can be every bit as sweet – at least that's how it happened for my mother. Even as a little girl, playing with her doll's pram in Schonortli, she knew she wanted a family of her own one day, but by the time she arrived in London – a beautiful, talented young designer with so much to prove – she was beginning to realise that the family she had always dreamed of might not be so easy to find.

Working for Marucelli had been hugely rewarding, but also physically exhausting and, for a while, she had forgotten how to relax and enjoy herself. Being young had never been easy for my mother – she had been forced to grow up fast after the war and had spent most of her teenage years looking after her little sisters and helping Nonna around the house. Nonno was a strict disciplinarian who wanted the best for his children, and any spare time she had was dedicated to school work and music lessons. It was a sound upbringing and she was grateful for the opportunities her parents had given her, but it meant that she had missed something important along the way: an element of fun, that she hoped to find in London.

With her thick dark brown hair, slender frame and fine Mediterranean features, my mother was easily as beautiful as the models she had worked with and she was looking forward to spending her wages on the micro minis and knee-length boots that she had seen in fashion magazines and knew were fast becoming every young girl's weekend uniform. But for that, she would need to find a job.

She arrived in England in 1963, a time of change when the respectable Fifties had been replaced by something edgier, more dangerous

She arrived in England in 1963, a time of change when the respectable Fifties had been replaced by something edgier, more dangerous. The fashion industry was ready to burst out of its tailored seams and take every self-respecting Catholic girl, like my mother, with it. She loved the freedom, but found it a little overwhelming at first and wondered what Nonna would say if she could see these English girls with their beehive hair styles and baby-doll dresses.

She spent her first few weeks in England at a language school in Bournemouth and rented a room there with a sculptor and his wife. It was a gentle introduction to life abroad, but made finding work in London all the more challenging. She took the train in as often as she could, buying a copy of the *Evening Standard* and circling all the design assistant jobs she could see, but it was swiftly eating away at her savings and she was eager to start earning. Then she saw a position for a junior designer at a large ready-to-wear factory in the West End called London Maid. The last girl had walked out under a cloud and they were desperate to fill her shoes quickly so they could meet their summer deadlines. She was introduced to the chief designer – a dashingly good-looking man with a mischievous glint in his eye and the sort of debonair charm she had always imagined Englishmen to have. He took a quick glance at her portfolio and offered her the job there and then, giving her two days to find somewhere to live. That was the first time my mother met my father and she wondered if he was always so confident: he had offered her a meagre sum of money, barely enough to live on, which he now claims was part of a master plan to coax her into having dinner with him every night.

My father on a business trip to New York in the 1940s

It was time for some home cooking and she grabbed her bag and went in search of the one thing she knew would make her feel better — chocolate

The next day she found a tiny bedsit in Knightsbridge, overlooking the back entrance to Harrods, and went and bought herself some work clothes. Suddenly Milan seemed very far away and as she sat, staring at the walls and thinking of Nonna and Nonno, she started to cry, longing for the familiar smells and sounds of Italy. It was time for some home cooking and she grabbed her bag and went in search of the one thing she knew would make her feel better — chocolate. A batch of Omama's Weinacht Guezi, even though it was the middle of summer, was enough to make her alien little room seem lived-in, and she sat by the window ledge and ate them, looking at the busy street below and feeling reassured.

The job turned out to be a godsend. It was hard work but not too intimidating and she found in her new colleagues a surrogate family. They were all much older than her, most of them of Polish or Russian descent, like my father, and there were some excellent designers and tailors, all craftsmen like my grandpa Sam Kalinsky and my father's great friend Silvia Michaels, who understood what it was like to be a foreigner in a strange city and took my mother under their wing.

Before long, she had settled into her new life, but she still desperately wanted to be a part of the throbbing crowds who shopped on the King's Road every Saturday, like the women who she saw there — dressed in their Mary Quant shifts with colourful tights and little patent court shoes. It was an exciting time and she would write home to Corrado and her sisters, telling them what music young people were listening to in London and feeling like a teenager again.

One thing she was quickly learning was that what the city had to offer in art and culture, it lacked in good-quality cooking. Restaurants had no idea how to make Italian food and the pasta was tough and bland, especially when topped with dry processed cheese. She had yet to find a shop which sold real Parmigiano Reggiano or the wonderful cakes and pastries she had been used to in Switzerland. To make matters worse, she had only one electric ring in her room, which made it difficult to prepare both pasta and sauce. Plain white pasta didn't exactly warm her heart, and she was beginning to despair when she met Gabrielle. A fellow Italian, she was living in one of the bedsits above my mother's and she too was craving a bowl of spaghetti Napoli. They got chatting, instantly finding comfort in familiarity, and agreed to cook together, my mother making the spaghetti and Gabrielle the sauce. They met on the stairs and ate it, laughing at the thought of two little Italian girls alone in such a big city.

They soon became firm friends and every Saturday, Gabrielle and my mother joined the crowds and headed for Biba, the most popular clothes shop at the time, on Kensington High Street. There they spent their week's wages on new make-up, bags, boots and tiny dresses, all the things they would never have dreamt of wearing at home in Italy.

At night, they would sit in my mother's bedroom, chewing on Omama's biscuits and watching for celebrities going into Harrods for some late-night shopping. My mother tells me now, with suitable drama, that one time they even saw a royal fleet of cars draw up and Princess Margaret get out, shielded by an entourage of attentive aides.

It wasn't long though before my mother seemed to have lost all interest in food: she had constant butterflies and felt nervous and sick when she went to work. She told Gabrielle, who looked at her friend and laughed: 'You're in love, darling,' she said and my mother knew she was right. She had known it from the moment she set eyes on my father and yet somehow it had still taken her by surprise. They had been spending a lot of time together and he had even been taking her with him to the fashion shows in Paris, treating her to expensive meals at night and teaching her all he knew about the 'rag trade', as he called it. Love was exactly what she had always dreamed it would be and she allowed herself to be swept up in the romance of it all, happy to let him spoil her with gifts and clothes that he had designed himself and had specially made.

At night, they would sit in my mother's bedroom, chewing on Omama's biscuits and watching for celebrities going into Harrods for some late-night shopping

Being Jewish and divorced, not to mention quite a bit older than my mother, the union was never going to sit well with Nonno, who was a proud Catholic and suspicious of this 'foreign' man's intentions. But my mother and father continued to see each other none the less, and in a short time my mother could barely remember what life had been like before. He knew all the best spots in London and took her to an Italian restaurant in Soho called Terrazza, which actually knew how to make food taste like food and was a favourite haunt for big-name stars like Marlon Brando, Sophia Loren and Frank Sinatra.

In Paris they ate at Le Dôme in Montparnasse, where it is said Sartre used to eat, with its little alcoves decorated with cinema pictures and an expensive arty feel. The atmosphere was as exquisite as the food and my mother, by then an excellent cook herself and always on the lookout for inspiration, ordered the Gateau l'Opéra. It was so good she spent ages eating it, and hours over the coming weeks trying to make it on her little cooking ring at home. It's a glorious concoction which almost warrants the time it takes to prepare. I have made it, only once, for a clothes-swap party at my friend Em's house and it took me almost an entire day. If you feel brave enough to attempt it, I would suggest making two simple cocoa cakes, layering them with dark chocolate ganache and covering the whole thing in a shiny chocolate glaze. I decorated mine with dried figs which I'd soaked in a sugar and lemon syrup and dusted with a tiny amount of edible gold leaf.

They were married in London in 1967 and even though it wasn't the big white church wedding my mother had always dreamed of, it was the happiest day of her life.

My parents had the best year of their lives while they were courting, going out every night: eating in the little Fountain restaurant at Fortnum and Mason's after the theatre, watching the ballet and opera together and exploring the parts of London where my father had grown up. They were married in London in 1967 and even though it wasn't the big white church wedding my mother had always dreamed of, it was the happiest day of her life. She was an Englishman's wife now, with new English friends, but she showed her wedding guests that she was still an Italian at heart the only way she knew how – by ordering an Italian-style chocolate wedding cake. I have always loved the idea of a chocolate sponge with white icing for a special occasion and, if my husband hadn't liked fruit cake so much, I might have convinced him to have one on our wedding day. The Italian wedding cakes are simple sponges with frilly white icing; sometimes the cake mix has some candied fruit inside. I have made it for special occasions and like it moist and simple. I use Omama's chocolate cake recipe, the same one that Nonna copied out of her green book when she was married and made for Nonno so many times.

My parents' wedding, 1967. Left to right: Grandpa, Grandma, my father, my mother, Nonna, Corrina, Nonno.

SCHOKOLADENTORTE –
OMAMA'S SPECIAL OCCASION CHOCOLATE CAKE

150 g (5½ oz) dark chocolate
280 g (10 oz) caster sugar
150 g (5½ oz) unsalted butter
5 eggs, separated
150 g (5½ oz) plain flour
1 teaspoon baking powder
50 g (1¾ oz) zucca (candied pumpkin)
50 g (1¾ oz) candied angelica

Preheat the oven to Gas Mark 4/180°C/fan oven 160°C.

Melt the chocolate in a bain-marie and add the sugar, butter and egg yolks. Mix well, then stir in the sifted flour and baking powder.

Whisk the whites until stiff and fold into the mixture with the candied fruit.

Put into a greased and lined 20-cm (8-inch) cake tin and bake for 45 minutes or until the cake comes away from the sides of the tin.

For a special occasion, decorate with white royal icing.

Nonno could see how happy his daughter was and accepted my father – though when England beat Italy in the World Cup the year they married, relations cooled off again for a while. My brother, Jem, was born a year later and now, nearly 40 years on, my mother still talks of that first year with my father as one of the happiest times of her life.

PART TWO:

Chocolate

&Memories

CHAPTER 7:

Praline for Lunch

istory has a habit of repeating itself in my family. When Nonna left her home in Switzerland to start a new life with Nonno in Milan, she couldn't have foreseen that her daughter and granddaughter would both one day do the same. Three generations of women, each of us deeply attached to our homes and families, but headstrong and independent enough to follow our hearts elsewhere. And just as our lives would follow similar paths, so too would our taste buds.

When I was nearly five, the age my mother was when Nonna led her on that wartime escape over the mountains, I was given my first Cailler praline finger – the same chocolate bar that my mother was given by Opapa at the end of their ordeal. It was on a similar journey too, over the mountains from Italy to Switzerland. I can't pretend the circumstances were anything like as dramatic, but the pleasure of eating that delightful Alpine chocolate treat was every bit as good.

Nonno would tell us this story every year, no doubt hoping it would one day encourage his little Anita to come home for good

We had just spent two idyllic weeks in the medieval coastal resort of Fiascherino on the Italian Riviera di Levante and were about to head on to Schonortli with my mother. My father only had a few precious weeks off a year, so our family holiday was usually just the four of us, all keen to make the most of our time together. But that year, my mother had offered to take our cousins Silvia and Laura with us too, giving her brother Corrado and his wife, my aunt Satu, some time alone with their eldest daughter, Cristina. For Jem and me, it was a welcome treat to have some extra playmates and my mother, who was also Silvia's *madrina* (godmother), was looking forward to spending some time with her little nieces.

Usually, Italians are eager to escape the oppressive heat of summer and they often head north in July and August. But Nonno had always impressed on his children the importance of good sea air and a healthy dose of sunshine for building up immunities to winter colds and childhood illnesses. He claimed the sun had saved his life when he was a boy and refused to hear a bad word said against it.

He must have been around seven or eight years old when he contracted tuberculosis. His parents didn't have the money to send him to the mountains to convalesce, as they would have liked, so instead they took him to stay with an uncle at the seaside. They were afraid the thick, salty air might do him more harm than good, but to their enormous relief it worked wonders. Before long, the colour was back in his cheeks and he was off making sandcastles with his cousins. Nonno would tell us this story every year, no doubt hoping it would one day encourage his little Anita to come home for good.

Fiascherino is one of those unspoilt little coastal resorts which allow you a glimpse of what Italy must have been like centuries ago. The buildings are in the style of the Cinque Terre, literally the Five Lands: rugged medieval stone houses, separated by narrow alleyways. D.H. Lawrence lived in the bay from 1913 to 1914 and once wrote that there was an ancient sadness to the olive groves and holm oak trees on the hillside terraces. I was too young to appreciate the poetic history which surrounded me, but my parents loved the area and had already spent wonderful holidays in nearby Lerici and Elba.

We were staying in a simple pensione, set in a shady pine wood, about half an hour's walk from the beach. There was a bus which went almost all the way, but in true laid-back Italian style it was usually late and sometimes didn't show up at all. So instead, we got up early each morning, packed a small picnic bag and trooped off. Silvia, who loved to swim and was very proud, even then, of her year-round Italian suntan, would tug at my father's arm, encouraging him to hurry up with impatient cries of '*Andiamo al'mare, Zio Harry*' (Let's go to the beach, Uncle Harry). The walk there was alongside a busy main road and we would sing our favourite marching songs to work up a good rhythm. I still remember carrying my little jelly beach-sandals and a bucket and spade, skipping on the hot gravel as I tried to keep up with Silvia and my mother. As soon as we arrived, dusty, sticky and a little frayed, we were more than ready for a dip in the sea. The colour of the water there was something I will never forget, a violet-blue so translucent it made you feel you could bend right down and drink it from cupped hands. While my parents laid out the towels, we ran in, splashing each other until we were drenched.

The beach always emptied at lunchtime, when most Italians went home for their siesta, but we gathered our picnic things and went and ate our panini in the shade of a little rocky cove. Jem had discovered the spot with my mother on our first day there and they had christened it 'Shell Corner' after the bed of broken shells which lined the ground. It was one of those enchanting little holiday hideaways, small, deserted and perfect for playing 'pirates' in. Jem stood on one of the high rocks with Laura, pretending it was a crow's nest, and they busied themselves 'keeping watch' while Silvia and I helped lay out the food and drink.

I still believe there is an art to preparing a good picnic and my mother seemed to have a knack for always

The colour of the water there was something I will never forget, a violet-blue so translucent it made you feel you could bend right down and drink it from cupped hands

packing the right things. We had our trusty brown and white thermos flask, which went everywhere with us, filled with watered-down juice or thick Italian fruit nectar, which we guzzled greedily. There was a panini each, with ham, Swiss cheese and fresh greens and herbs from the surrounding hills, and a big crescent of watermelon for dessert. Sometimes we would have a slice of pizza bianca, focaccia sprinkled with rosemary and sea salt, which my mother bought fresh from the *fornaio* on the way and, always when we were least expecting it, she would pack a little surprise for us children. Our favourites were delicious vanilla wafers filled with nutty chocolate cream or the Italian chocolate eggs which always came with free toys inside, although we usually spent more time arguing about who had the best toy than we did eating them.

I still pack a little chocolate surprise when I go on picnics with my family and have convinced myself that these Chocolate Florentine Bars, while not actually being terribly healthy, at least sound as if they are. The children love the nuts and glacé cherries, and the real fun, as with all children's sweets, is in the wrapping. I use something different each time but my son, being a bit of a magpie, loves silver foil and ribbon best.

CHOCOLATE FLORENTINE BARS —
FOR LITTLE WALKERS

100 g (3¹/₂ oz) golden syrup
75 g (2³/₄ oz) unsalted butter
50 g (1³/₄ oz) light brown sugar
50 g (1³/₄ oz) glacé cherries, chopped
85 g (3 oz) candied mixed peel
50 g (1³/₄ oz) raisins or sultanas
70 g (2¹/₂ oz) almonds, chopped
25 g (1 oz) pistachio nuts, roughly chopped
100 g (3¹/₂ oz) plain flour
200 g (7 oz) milk chocolate

Preheat the oven to Gas Mark 4/180°C/fan oven 160°C.

Heat the golden syrup, butter and sugar in a heavy-bottomed pan until the sugar has dissolved.

Remove from the heat and add the fruits and nuts. Stir well, then sift in the flour.

Grease and line an 18 x 28-cm (7 x 11-inch) baking tray and pour the mixture in, smoothing it with a palette knife. Bake for 20 minutes or until golden brown, then set aside to cool.

Melt the chocolate in a bain-marie.

Cut the cooled mixture into small bars, about 2.5 cm (1 inch) long, and dip each one into the melted chocolate to coat the base well. Place on a sheet of greaseproof paper to set.

When the chocolate has hardened, wrap each bar in some foil paper and tie with pink and blue ribbons.

Makes about 15

When it was time to go, without the promise of a cool, refreshing swim at the end of our walk, it was harder to muster enthusiasm. To raise our spirits, my parents would promise us each an ice cream in the piazza when we got back. It was only a tiny square – just big enough for one café with a few little tables outside and a regular clientele of locals, drinking granita or wine from the local vineyards and playing *Scopa* in the afternoon sun. But the café served the best ice creams I had ever tasted: rich, thick and tooth-tinglingly sweet. I always chose pistachio and chocolate and had a struggle to lick it faster than it was melting. Toni, the ice cream man, had a bit of a soft spot for Jem and me. We had rehearsed how to say '*Un gelato e un bichier d'acqua, per favore*' (One ice cream and a glass of water, please) in our cute English accents and he usually slipped us a little almond biscotto when my mother wasn't looking.

I have always thought that pistachio and chocolate complement each other beautifully and love baking a batch of those hard teatime biscotti with some bitter cocoa powder and fresh pistachio nuts instead of almonds. Biscotti, like its French counterpart 'biscuit', means twice cooked, a technique which gives the Italian teatime treats their distinctive crunch and hard texture. As a child, the nuances of this meaning were lost on me – however, it now serves as a useful reminder to always put them back in the oven for an authentic finish.

They are extremely easy to make and look just like the ones you buy in the shops. A few of these, dipped in dark chocolate, make the perfect gift – with a bottle of vinsanto or a packet of freshly ground Italian coffee.

'TONI'S TREATS' –
CHOCOLATE & PISTACHIO BISCOTTI

300 g (10½ oz) plain flour
70 g (2½ oz) cocoa powder
1 teaspoon baking powder
220 g (7½ oz) caster sugar
250 g (9 oz) whole shelled pistachio nuts
3 eggs
2 teaspoons amaretto

Sift the flour, cocoa powder and baking powder, then add the sugar and nuts.

Whisk the eggs with the amaretto and fold into the mixture until it forms a hard dough.

Roll into two long fat sausages and wrap in clingfilm. Chill in the refrigerator for 30 minutes.

Preheat the oven to Gas Mark 4/180°C/fan oven 160°C and bake the logs for 30 minutes, or until firm.

Cool on a rack, then cut diagonally into biscotti and rebake at Gas Mark 1/140°C /fan oven 120°C for a further 25 minutes.

Cool and dust with cocoa powder.

Serve with pistachio ice cream and a small glass of vinsanto.

Makes about 30

At home, my father worked long hours and was often away on business trips – attending fashion shows in Paris or meeting with cloth agents and buyers all over Europe – so to have him to ourselves for two weeks a year was something Jem and I eagerly looked forward to. He loved the time he had with us too, and spent most of it teaching us how to draw. There is a pride children feel for their parents, an unwavering, innocent certainty that they can do everything better than anyone else. I'm sure my friends must have grown quite bored hearing how my mother's jewellery was the best in the world and her sketches the most accurate, and of course her birthday cakes were better than anything you could buy in the shops. Everything she touched turned to gold in my eyes and the same was true of my father, especially when he had a pen in his hand.

There is a pride children feel for their parents, an unwavering, innocent certainty that they can do everything better than anyone else

I loved nothing better than to watch him draw – quick, bold lines on a page which captured a mood in moments – and wherever we went when we were little, he was always sketching ideas on the back of restaurant napkins or old street maps. I loved to copy him, learning how to create a scene in just a few lines, and as soon as I was old enough to hold a pencil, he began teaching me all the tricks he had picked up over the years. He is well into his eighties now, but his fashion designs from the Thirties and Forties were once much sought after and one of his original sketch pads is still on display at the Victoria and Albert Museum in London.

On that holiday, my father would take Jem and me and our cousins down to the little harbour in Tellaro in the evenings, when the light was gentle and muted but still clear enough to see what you were doing. We would all sit in a row and draw until the sun went down, listening to the peaceful lapping of the water and the distant sound of children playing in the piazza. The painting he later did of those little wooden fishing boats still hangs on the dining room wall in my parents' house, but he gave me the line drawing and I take it with me everywhere, a reminder of those balmy summer evenings almost 30 years ago.

The afternoons in Italy are a quiet family time, when most restaurants and *tabaccherias* close for a few hours. I love the atmosphere in the streets during the 'siesta hours' when all you can hear is the gentle mewing of stray cats in the tiny *vincoli* and the sound of dishes clinking as people do their washing-up after lunch. My parents would take advantage of that time to read or sketch on the balcony, leaving us children to amuse ourselves. I loved being with my cousins, which was like having two older sisters to play with, and I remember making rose water with Laura, using petals from the wood and mixing them with water from a rusty outside tap. We spent hours playing at being famous film stars, dabbing our necks with the expensive '*eau de toilette*' and taking it in turns to teeter about in my mother's high-heeled white sandals.

But our favourite pastime was collecting *pinoli*, delicious, creamy pine nuts, which lined the ground and made for the ideal after-lunch snack. We sat cross-legged and content, cracking the hard shells with stones and munching away until it was nearly dark. Pine nuts are so expensive to buy that we hardly ever had them as children, so to be able to feast on as many as I could physically manage was a real luxury. Now, I use them to add crunch to hazelnut meringues, or sometimes at Christmas, for authentic Panforte Nero. But then I just ate them fresh, enjoying them so much I barely noticed the black sooty dust their shells were leaving on my hands and sundress.

I make these light teatime meringues in the summer, when I'm missing Italy most, and usually serve them with a bitter chocolate sauce. But they are just as good filled with sweet chocolate cream and decorated with a sprinkling of icing sugar.

> *Pine nuts are so expensive to buy that we hardly ever had them as children, so to be able to feast on as many as I could physically manage was a real luxury*

PINE NUT MERINGUES WITH RICH CHOCOLATE SAUCE

3 egg whites
200 g (7 oz) vanilla sugar (page 242)
1 tablespoon ground hazelnuts
100 g (3½ oz) pine nuts

For the chocolate sauce
200 g (7 oz) bitter dark chocolate
85 g (3 oz) unsalted butter
a pinch of ground cloves

Preheat the oven to Gas Mark 1/140°C/fan oven 120°C.

Whisk the egg whites in a clean bowl until stiff. Add the sugar and hazelnuts slowly, whisking as you go until it has all been mixed in and the meringue is stiff and glossy. Fold in the pine nuts.

Spoon small dollops of the mixture on to a prepared baking tray. Bake for 1½ hours, or until dry and crisp.

To make the sauce, simply melt the chocolate in a bain-marie and add the butter and cloves, stirring until it has all dissolved.

Serve the sauce hot, poured over the meringues.

Makes about 25

When it was time to leave, I filled my suitcase with bags of the pine nuts, which my mother would use for her Pesto alla Genovese when we got home. The basil which grows on the hills all along the coast to Genoa is ideal for this rich and versatile sauce, which I still find extremely relaxing to make, especially if you take the time to pound the leaves in a mortar and pestle. I sometimes eat spoonfuls of fresh pesto on its own, straight from the bowl, but it's wonderful with orecchietti or to add flavour to a minestrone in winter. My mother never bothered with exact measurements, using a generous bunch of fresh, unbruised basil with about 1½ tablespoons of crushed pine nuts, 1 tablespoon each of grated peccorino and Parmigiano Reggiano and a good drizzle of olive oil. Try, if you can, to find out where you can buy olive oil fresh. Just pressed, it has a wonderfully fragrant taste and scent which can be a little too aromatic for some dishes, but is perfect for pesto.

At the end of our holiday in Fiascherino, my mother was to take us children on to Switzerland by train, while my father returned to his job back home. Corrado and Satu would be waiting for us in Schonortli with Cristina and Nonna and Nonno, who would have driven from their apartment in Milan at the start of the summer. When Omama died in 1969, rather than leave Schonortli to any one person she had asked that her children draw lots for it. Nonna won, but of course the house remained a family holiday home for everyone to share and we all enjoyed getting together there once a year.

'Yonta, yonta', my word for 'I want some, I want some'

Jem and I had been going to Schonortli since we were babies, and my earliest memory of the trip there was being given a milk chocolate bar by one of the air stewardesses on the Swissair flight. It had a picture of the Alps on the wrapping and I can still remember how it tasted now – of sweet cocoa butter and milk.

Even as a child, I always loved to eat. My parents tell me I was so eager for my evening ice cream in Italy, I would yell: 'Yonta, yonta', my word for 'I want some, I want some', until somebody took pity on me. And I will never forget our waiter at the little trattoria we sometimes went to for pasta at lunchtime in Fiascherino. He was a small, wiry teenager with a toothy grin and oily black hair who was amazed at how much food a five-year-old could manage. He would hover nervously over my plate, asking:

'*Va bene cosi?*' (Is that enough?) as he dished out my favourite trenette, large spaghetti with tomatoey sugo. But each time I stubbornly shook my head until he had piled my plate so high, I could barely see over the top.

I loved Italy as a girl and now, more than ever, I miss those lazy holidays eating creamy gelati in the piazzas and munching on crunchy amaretti biscuits while my parents drank coffee, but there was something magical about Switzerland in summer and I spent my last few days in Fiascherino excitedly looking forward to my 'second holiday'. I dreamed greedily of the shop windows in Berne and Thun which would be filled with honeyed gingerbread, brightly wrapped chocolate bars and huge marzipan fruits.

I dreamed greedily of the shop windows in Berne and Thun which would be filled with honeyed gingerbread, brightly wrapped chocolate bars and huge marzipan fruits

But getting there was another matter. It was peak holiday season and the only train tickets my mother could get were for 15 August – *ferragosto*. This is one of the biggest, most important religious festivals in Italy and the busiest time to travel. My mother knew it would be a long and boring journey so she packed our little rucksacks with cioccolatini and bought us each a Toppolino, a thick, Mickey Mouse cartoon book, to keep us entertained. But before long, she realised it wouldn't be enough. The first leg of the journey, to Milan, should have taken only four hours, but there were strikes on the line and it had taken at least six. To make matters worse, our carriage was full and a family from the south of Italy had decided to sit in our seats. Even though my mother pleaded with them to move, they refused and we had no choice but to sit on our suitcases and watch as they opened their lunch parcels and began eating strong-smelling salami and drinking wine.

Before long, the smell of their food made me feel queasy and I could feel myself about to erupt into a flood of tears. Just then, I felt a tap on my shoulder. Looking up, I saw a kind-looking man smiling down at me. I watched silently as he reached his hand out to me and could see that he was holding a brightly wrapped sweet, which he offered with a gentle nod. I looked at my mother for approval and she told me to take it and say thank you. '*Bitte schon*', I said in a quiet voice, having learnt the phrase for when we arrived in Switzerland. The man smiled and I unwrapped my prize. It looked a little like a small twig, brown and knobbly. I was cautious at first, but as soon as I bit into it I felt my spirits lift. The milk chocolate was thick and creamy and had already started melting on to my fingers. I ate quickly, keen not to waste any of it.

That was my first Cailler praline bar and it was just what I needed, a sweet diversion. When I had finished, I folded the red foil wrapping and put it in my pocket, vowing to keep it for ever – just as my mother had done nearly 30 years before me. I leant contentedly against her leg and, before long, I was fast asleep, dreaming of picnics in the mountains and fruit-picking with my cousins.

CHAPTER 8:

Landhaus Schonortli

*I*t was nearly dark by the time we stepped off the train in Thun, or at least that's how I remember it. A winter's palette of purple and mauve and twilight blue filled the sky and a few ominous drops of rain reminded us that we had left Italy behind. The effect of the praline bar had begun to wear off and we were all in need of some cheer. Fortunately, my uncle Corrado was just the person to provide it, and the moment I saw him pull up in Nonno's old Mercedes, our 'Schonortli car', I knew we would be all right. Soon, he had Jem and me in fits of giggles, shouting 'Hello, honey' to my mother in an exaggerated American accent and howling theatrically when Laura jumped up at him.

Corrado always ran at life with an energy which was both invigorating and contagious. He ate quickly as though the food in front of him might suddenly be taken away, walked with a nervous skip in his step, and drove like my mother when she had an open road and a good manual car – fast. I gripped tightly on to Jem's hand in the back seat as we sped through the winding roads leading up to Schonortli, while Corrado and my mother spoke in animated Italian to each other, eager to catch up on a year's news in 10 minutes.

Schonortli

It was always a comfort to see that nothing had changed from the previous year. We drove through Thun, with its cobbled streets and fairy-tale castle, to Oberhofen. I loved the sleepy, tidy little town with its tiny windsurfing club and a restaurant which served excellent Bratwurst and onions, just like my mother made back home when she was feeling nostalgic. I still eat it now with potato rosti on cold cardigan-days in England. I make it just like my mother used to, frying the sausages in a pan with some sliced onions and a sprinkling of caster sugar and moulding the grated potatoes into flat patties to shallow fry.

I thought of the sweet shops and patisseries in Berne, their windows filled with tempting cakes and tarts and decorated with biscuit bears and marzipan fruits

Schonortli was only a short drive from Oberhofen and as we reached the foot of the dense wood which surrounded it, I could feel my stomach flutter with excitement. I have often wondered what I miss most about it now and I think it would have to be the mountains: the proud Eiger; the majestic Jungfrau; the Stockhorn which we had walked on so many times – they were always there to greet us, like old friends welcoming us home. Each room in the house had a plaque bearing the name of the view from its balcony and sometimes my mother would come and look out with me in the evenings, showing me the light at the top of the Niesen and telling me it was a restaurant. I would go to bed that night imagining people dining there, dancing a waltz under the stars and looking back at us.

As I listened to Corrado, trying to pick out the odd word of Italian understood, I thought of the sweet shops and patisseries in Berne, their windows filled with tempting cakes and tarts and decorated with biscuit bears and marzipan fruits. I pictured myself walking up the hill from Schonortli at sunset to collect the milk from Frau Amstutz's farm, and later drinking it cold with cocoa and sugar before bed in my favourite nursery teacup. I thought of sleeping that night in my holiday room – the one on the top floor which had story-book wallpaper and the best view of the Eiger. I imagined lying in the high wooden bed, looking at the pictures of the Pied Piper of Hamelin, a little snake of children behind him, winding their way across the walls. My cousins and Jem slept in the rooms either side of mine and I smiled at the memory of shouting out '*buona notte*' insincerely to them and then creeping into one of their rooms once our parents were in bed. Nonna and Nonno slept directly below us, but we had perfected the art of tiptoeing between the creaks in the floorboards and would sometimes sit for ages before someone came to order us back to bed.

Illustration from my favourite nursery teacup, featuring Max and Moritz (Max und Moritz: eine Bubengeschichte in sieben Streichen (Max and Moritz: a juvenile history in seven tricks) by Wilhelm Busch, Munchen, Braun und Schneider, 1925)

I realised then that what I loved so much about Schonortli was that it was our place. Our heights were marked on the wall in the kitchen, they were our toys in the cupboards and our pictures on the walls. That safe familiarity was its charm, and its gift to us were the memories we made while we were there – usually sitting around the dinner table, eating cheese fondue or Nonna's Napoleon's Torte and fighting over who had the biggest slice. Even though the house is no longer ours, those happy memories are, a sweet-tasting legacy we will one day pass on to our children and grandchildren.

My mother once told me she felt sad that no one in England would ever really know the true Anita, the one who loved to play at being a nurse or who used to put her cardigan on her head and pretend she was a fairy-tale princess. But for me, that little girl is still there and comes out every time she is with her family. Schonortli let me see that side of her too and I will always be grateful to it for that. I remember watching with pride as she played duets on the piano with Silvia, climbed the trees in the garden with Jem and cooked traditional Swiss and Italian dishes with Satu in the kitchen. I wished more than anything that my father could see her there more often – I knew if he did he would fall in love with her all over again each time.

She taught me so much about life and how to live it on those holidays, but I think the greatest lesson I learnt from her then was how to use my imagination. Instead of reading stories to Jem and me, she would give us paper on which to write our own. With our crayons and coloured pencils, we created whole worlds, peopled with the characters in her bedtime *favole* – fairy tales she had grown up on and used to tell us each night before we went to sleep.

I suppose what I loved most about my mother then was her ability to make ordinary things seem special. Sugar became

Corrado playing chess with Laura and Cristina in the Haxihus

delicious, spoon-bending caramel to line her crème caramel pots, eggs were whipped into meringues or creamy zabaglione, and sandwiches became an unrivalled pleasure when they had just a few pieces of bitter dark chocolate inside. She had sweet sorcery in her blood, I'm sure of it, and she claims it all started – that desire of hers to make an adventure of life – in Schonortli.

Opapa's beautiful Victorian summer house on the lake of Thun had been her childhood place of escape. Lying in bed in her room in Milan, listening to the soft breathing of her two sisters as they slept, she would close her eyes tightly and try to picture the enchanting chalet where she spent her summers. She imagined she could reach out and touch the little wooden swing which hung from one of the oak trees in the garden. The higher she went in it, the more she could see of the mountains – their snow-topped peaks such a comfort after the rubble and dust of the streets of Milan. Closing her eyes tighter still, she could almost smell the ripe fruit from the apple trees and berry orchard near the house. And, if she tried really hard, she believed she was skipping along one of the shady forest paths leading down to the lake and jumping into the icy mountain water.

There was most definitely a magic to Schonortli. I felt it too when I was a girl, running down the same corridors as my mother had run down, playing with the same toys in the *Spielzimmer*, and falling asleep to the same lulling sound of foghorns on the lake at night. Those happy memories, which had seeped into the walls over the years, had breathed life into the old house and, from the minute I stepped through the thick wooden door, I felt I was travelling back in time to when my mother was a girl.

The name Schonortli means 'beautiful little spot' in Swiss German. Opapa had bought the house on the same day that my mother was born. To celebrate, he painted her birth date and four little hearts on one of the walls in the *Haxihus* in the garden. These Swiss playhouses, literally translated the name means 'witch's house', are common all over the Bernese Oberland. Sometimes built to look like miniature versions of the main house and painted with fairy-tale murals, they provide the perfect hideaway for little children and a welcome protection from the frequent late summer thunderstorms.

Ours had a circular bench inside and a red table for our toy cups and saucers. Over the years, the sour cherry trees around it grew to provide the perfect canopy from the rain, and sometimes Silvia and I were allowed our afternoon *merenda* in there. This Italian answer to an afterschool snack was often the highlight of my day. At home in England Jem and I were always allowed a slice of toast and jam or one of my mother's chocolate sandwiches at teatime, but in Schonortli we ate little bars of milk chocolate and listened to the water trickling down from the roof. I have often wondered if that was where I learnt to love chocolate and associate it with happy times. When we were back home in London, my mother taught Jem and me to make our own chocolate bars, which we ate in the garden, pretending we were all back in Schonortli.

MERENDA CHOCOLATE BARS

100 g (3½ oz) white chocolate
50 g (1¾ oz) glacé cherries, chopped
100 g (3½ oz) milk chocolate
50 g (1¾ oz) whole hazelnuts
a generous handful of raisins
50 g (1¾ oz) dark chocolate

Melt and temper the white chocolate (page 241) and fold in the glacé cherries. Pour the mixture on to a greased baking tray to set.

Do the same with the milk chocolate, adding the whole nuts and raisins.

When both mixtures are hard, cut them into little rectangles, about 5 cm (2 inches) long, with a sharp kitchen knife.

Melt the dark chocolate and drizzle over the white bars for decoration.

Wrap each one in foil and eat in the garden. (Sometimes we made Haxihus bars by drawing scenes from our favourite fairy tales on coloured paper and wrapping them around the foil.)

Makes about 6

I had to look hard to find my mother's birth date on the *Haxihus* wall when I was little, years of rain and harsh winds had weathered the paint and it was well hidden in the Hansel and Gretel mural, but for me it summed up the spirit of Schonortli – a place bought with love where our family could come together for a few special weeks each year.

When my mother was little, Omama loved to tell her stories about the house and its history. She said that the previous owner – a stout man with a neat handlebar moustache – had been a wealthy German diplomat and his wife a beautiful actress. 'They threw wonderful parties in the summer,' she would say dramatically, as my mother and Corrado sat cross-legged in front of her. 'She wore dresses sent from the fashion-houses of Paris and, it is said, she even had each button individually made for her with her initials embroidered on them.'

When my mother asked what their guests had to eat, Omama would look dreamily out over the lake, thinking back to the parties she used to throw for Opapa's clients at their home in Berne. 'There were large dishes of Prussiennes and delicious chocolate mousses, decorated with sweet whipped cream,' she would say, smiling down at her. Years later, Omama gave my mother that recipe for her chocolate mousse and told her to enjoy it with friends, as she had. Omama used to make it with only whipped cream and grated chocolate, the easiest thing in the world to prepare and perfect for a quick dessert. But over the years, my mother modified it slightly, adding egg yolks to the chocolate for a richer, thicker finish. I have included both versions here and still have trouble deciding which I prefer. I can still remember the delightful ceramic pots my mother used to serve it in. They were shaped like little barrels with dark brown enamelled handles on the side, which I thought looked just like the chocolate shapes she made to go on top for decoration. My father loved desserts when we were young and there were always a few of these in the fridge as they are so delicious and provide the perfect licking bowl for impatient children.

'There were large dishes of Prussiennes and delicious chocolate mousses, decorated with sweet whipped cream'

OMAMA'S CHOCOLATE MOUSSE

200 ml (7 fl oz) whipping cream
50 g (1³/₄ oz) dark chocolate, finely grated

Simply whip the cream until you can turn the bowl upside down and it doesn't move, then grate in the chocolate and fold in gently.

Serves 10

MY MOTHER'S CHOCOLATE MOUSSE

175 g (6 oz) dark chocolate
1 dessertspoon rum
3 eggs, separated
25 g (1 oz) unsalted butter
100 ml (3¹/₂ fl oz) double cream
a little icing sugar

Heat the chocolate and rum with 2–3 tablespoons of water. While it is still hot, add the egg yolks and chop in the butter. Stir well until the butter is melted.

Whisk the egg whites until stiff and stir in. Leave to cool, then chill in the refrigerator overnight.

When you are ready to eat, transfer the mousse into individual pots. Whip the cream with a little icing sugar and put a dollop on top of each one.

Serve with a rum granita.

Serves 8

My mother dressed in her favourite nurse's uniform

My mother and Satu used to do most of the cleaning and chores on our Schonortli 'holidays', a huge undertaking considering there were almost always at least ten of us staying there and goodness knows how many rooms to tidy. The only concession my cousins and I made to housework was to clean the *Spielzimmer* and help clear the table after dinner. But Omama told my mother that the previous owners had kept a number of servants who lived in the house all year round. They also employed Frau Kempf, from the little farmhouse next door, as their housekeeper and Herr Kempf, her husband, as coachman.

There was an old-fashioned bell-board mounted on the wall outside the kitchen with enamel buttons bearing the names of each of the rooms in the house. When the owners wanted something

they would ring, and a little light would flash on and off – there was even a button for the linden trees down by the berry orchard, which my mother used to call the 'linden bell'. One year, Silvia had flu and Satu told her to stay in bed and ring if she needed anything. On the first day, she rang only once, asking for a hot bowl of pastina – our cure-all chicken broth with pasta stars in it. On the second day she called twice for toast and jam, and on the third day she had us all running up and down the stairs with bowls of grapes, mugs of cocoa and vanilla biscuits – that was when Satu knew she was well enough to come back downstairs.

Of course Nonna and Nonno never normally used the bells, but there was a big brass gong at the foot of the stairs in the hallway which we all took turns to bang when meals were ready. Schonortli was three storeys high and yet wherever you were, you could always hear that familiar booming sound which meant that food was on the table.

When the gong sounded, we all came running, washing our hands in the little stone drinking fountain by the front door and helping to bring dishes to the table. Nonna, who was used to having a cook in Milan, would often draw up a weekly menu with my mother and Satu, and shopping trips became a military operation with one or other of them chauffeuring her to and from Thun for supplies. Lunch was the biggest meal of the day, starting with spaghetti – which Nonno taught Jem and I to twirl so that

none of the strands fell off our forks – followed by a schnitzel or bistecca and vegetable contorno. Dinner was much simpler: a big bowl of Bircher muesli – breakfast cereal with nuts and raisins topped with fresh yogurt – or Hernli, which we ate with grated Emmenthal and some cold meats and cheeses. The most common Italian dessert for any meal is *frutta fresca* (fresh fruit), or my mother often prepared a Kuchen – one of our favourite fruit flans which we ate with pouring cream and sugar.

We also ate a lot of Swiss dishes, making best use of the local produce and customs. On festivals and special occasions, we made a big cheese fondue and ate it with a bowl of forfeits on the table for anyone unlucky enough to drop their bread in the bowl. If it was cold and stormy outside, Corrado sometimes prepared a raclette, heating the hard Swiss cheese over the fire and cutting it into paper-thin slices which we ate with baked potatoes and sweet gherkins. If people came to stay, we would sometimes have a Bernerteller – a cold meat platter made with cured hams and Nonna's favourite, Bundnerfleisch, a salty air-dried beef which is delicious with big vine tomatoes.

One of my favourite chores was collecting fruit for dinner, and most evenings Silvia and I walked down to the linden trees together to pick *mirtilli* (bilberries). There was usually rain in the air in August – a cool moistness which made us walk with a spring in our step so we wouldn't get caught in an impromptu downpour.

I loved that time, when all you could hear were the cowbells in the distance and the sound of crickets in the tall grass. We took little straw baskets from one of the cupboards in the kitchen and filled them with the ripe berries, sometimes picking a red apple each from our neighbour's trees while we were there and munching it on the way home.

I loved that time, when all you could hear were the cowbells in the distance and the sound of crickets in the tall grass

Corrado never sat down to the table without a tall glass of cold milk in front of him, and fruit always tasted better when it came with some fresh pouring cream, so on our way back from 'the linden', Silvia and I would go and fetch a litre of each from Frau Amstutz's farm. She was a kindly woman with a white bun on the top of her head and gentle blue eyes – like Nonna's. She lived in a small chalet just up the hill from Schonortli, where she kept a few cows and some chickens and an Old English sheepdog which Laura and I had uncharitably christened '*cane cattiva*' (bad dog), after it once barked at us without warning! We ran along the path, rehearsing what we would say: '*Eine Liter, bitte*', with a winning smile, which we knew would award us a chocolate finger to share on the way home. When I was very little, Jem and I would also go to Herr Bigler's house near the linden trees for fresh eggs – just as my mother had done as a child – and the most delicious, chewy honeycomb honey I have ever tasted, which we all loved for breakfast in the mornings.

Being a small part of such a large family, there seemed to be an almost constant procession of first cousins, second cousins, aunts, uncles and family friends at Schonortli. Nonna would try to stagger the visitors, believing that small children shouldn't be over-excited, but sometimes they all just came at once anyway, bringing stories, toys for us children, and an excellent excuse to buy cakes from the Milk Bar in Oberhofen.

My family members are all such different characters, but what they share is a generosity of spirit and easy sense of fun, which have given me a wonderful guide by which to live my life. They each took me under their wing on those holidays and, together, taught me how to speak Italian, play their favourite tunes on the piano, crochet, knit, ski and swim. Nonna taught us about the mountains and Satu took Jem and me mushroom-picking in the woods; while, Rosalba showered us with warm love and affection, reminding us all how lucky we were to be a part of such a big Italian family.

CHAPTER 9:

Mrs Chocolate

When Opapa bought Schonortli, he wanted it to be a family home – a place where his children and grandchildren could come and relax, enjoying each other's company and learning about each other's lives. Silvia and I used to dream of owning a house just like it when we were older and living there with our own families all year round. Even though I missed my father a great deal on those holidays, there was a comforting warmth to being surrounded by so many of the people I loved, and I looked forward to seeing them all – hoping to learn a little more about my mother each time.

I discovered that she shares her striking physical beauty with Rosalba, who used to be an air hostess for Alitalia before she met and married my uncle Maurizio, and has Nonna's fine features and generous smile. Her daughter – our youngest cousin, Maria Isabella – was the little doll of the family, with her dark shiny ringlets and sparkling eyes and an irresistibly sweet nature.

My aunts Rosalba (left) and Corrina

My aunt Corrina, the youngest, shares my mother's naivety and enviable innocence. She is a lay nun in Milan and, when I was little, was always so busy with her charity work that I hardly saw her – which meant that when I did, I appreciated it all the more. Silvia, who sometimes visited her on school holidays, told me that she was the gentlest person, a small oasis of calm amid the heat and energy my family generated. '*E dolcissima*' (She is so sweet), Silvia would say, as we stood looking at the black and white picture of all four of them in Nonno's study.

Family stories were a bit like Chinese Whispers when I was little, with everyone phoning each other with news which changed a little each time as it filtered through Corrado, Rosalba and Nonna. By the time it reached us, it was usually so far removed from the truth we had to start right back at the beginning again. But at Schonortli, we had the luxury of hearing everything first hand.

Tante Greti, Nonna's eldest sister, sometimes came for tea, walking up the hill and through the wood from her chalet nearby with a stick in one hand and a shopping bag in the other. She told us about Nonna when she was little, smiling at us with the same watery eyes as our grandmother, and we would watch the sunset over the Alps together. My mother's cousin Hildi occasionally walked over with her dogs, and everyone got terribly excited. '*La Hi*,' they shouted through the corridors of Schonortli as Laura and Cristina prepared sandwiches and we laid out special cakes and pastries on the table outside. Hildi told Jem and me in perfect English how she had played by the linden trees with our mother when she was little, just as we did with our cousins, and we looked at pictures of them all, skinny little war children in their home-made knitted swimming trunks.

I murmured that the sugar would keep them awake for hours, but both she and my mother insisted chocolate was the best thing to give children before bed — to give them sweet dreams

But of all our visitors, it was my mother's youngest cousin, Franzi, who spoilt us the most. She loved to treat us and I still remember my joy at seeing her walk up the gravel path to greet us, bags of sweet goodies under each arm. Franzi has been a keen writer all her life, and she always used to remind me of a character in a story book, one of those who never had children of their own but loved to spoil other people's and seem always to have pockets full of enticing appetite-ruiners. Franzi is petite and bright-eyed with soft chestnut curls and has a distinctive laugh which reaches a high-pitched crescendo and then collapses, bubbling over like a mountain brook.

Each time she came she brought chocolate, and she still takes great pride in making sweet treats for her friends' children, covering ice-cream balls in hard white chocolate and calling them snow-topped mountains. She recently came to stay with us for Jem's wedding, bringing marzipan fruits for me and a bag full of chocolate ladybirds for my children. I murmured that the sugar would keep them awake for hours, but both she and my mother insisted chocolate was the best thing to give children before bed — to give them sweet dreams.

And nowhere has better chocolate than Switzerland. *Schokolade* is their national pride and joy and the Swiss eat almost 11 kilos of it each a year. The army gives conscripts free bars with the country's flag on the foil wrapping, and every canton has its own speciality, each trying to outdo the other. The result is a collection of weird and wonderful chocolate 'follies'. In the Jura, they make gift boxes containing chocolate wrist watches; Berne produces chocolate bears and cakes with the imprint of the canton's grizzly mascot on the front; and in Geneva you can buy chocolate cauldrons filled with marzipan vegetables. This unusual tradition dates back to the 17th century, when the Duke of Savoy's troops tried to attack the old walled city. A patriotic housewife, called Mère Royaume, threw a pot of scalding vegetable soup at them as they scaled the walls and now her bravery is commemorated with the city's famous Escalade festival in December, where shops make the sweet soup pots for tourists. The fun is in cracking the cauldron open like an Easter egg and finding all the marzipan fruits inside.

Franzi knew about all these chocolate delicacies and she would tell Jem and me about the seasonal displays in the windows of patisseries and chocolatiers in Berne. In autumn they would line marzipan meadows with chocolate mushrooms and sugar-coated pebbles, in spring chocolate Easter bunnies skipped among sugar flowers, and in winter there would be rows of gingerbread houses and chocolate presents under elaborate marzipan trees. Franzi brought them all to life for us, and our own Christmas tree at home was never complete without bags of chocolate coins and present-sacks which she sent well in advance.

My mother affectionately called her 'Mrs Chocolate', because whenever she came to meet us, it was always with a huge Merkur bag under her arm and a big, mischievous smile on her face

My mother affectionately called her 'Mrs Chocolate' when we were little, because whenever she came to meet us at Zurich airport, it was always with a huge Merkur bag under her arm and a big, mischievous smile on her face. Merkur is one of the best chocolate and sweet shops in Switzerland and she loved to treat us, bringing all the things she knew we couldn't get at home. She filled those bags with tiny fruit sweets called Sugus, which were soft and chewy and came in a rainbow of tempting colours. There were also slabs of honeyed spice bread, with the imprint of the Bernese bear on the front and white icing piped around the edge. When I asked Franzi for a recipe for it, she smiled and winked and leant in close: 'It's a secret you know,' she said in her wonderful accented English. There were the obligatory marzipan fruits and vegetables: carrots with authentic muddy ridges on the sides and peaches with glowing red blooms. One year, Franzi brought Silvia and me a chocolate ladybird each and a packet of chocolate pebbles with a crisp, sugar coating. We took them outside and played with them in the garden, hiding them among the real stones and laughing when we found them again.

Sometimes she brought sugar mice with chocolate noses and long tails, but the one thing we could always be sure of getting was chocolate. We had five bars each: a dark Lindt for cooking and a white one with crushed vanilla beans; milk chocolate with pistachio cream inside, which came in individual little pieces; and a milky praline so soft it tasted just like solidified cream, which is probably exactly what it was. But the best – the one we would have undoubtedly fought over if Franzi hadn't had the foresight to get us one each – was the Rayon bar which had been my mother's favourite as a girl and was fast becoming ours.

At home, Jem and I always looked forward to Franzi's sweet food parcels with greedy curiosity, eager for reminders of those happy Schonortli memories. One year she sent us all a parcel of Zuristei, which means 'stones from Zurich', and we must have eaten them within minutes of opening the box. They were gloriously indulgent little treats made with a thin pastry shell and filled with thick chocolate cream. I have tried to copy them at home, never quite getting the same taste but coming up with good imitations and certainly having a lot of fun in the process. You can fill them with chocolate custard, which is similar to the filling in the originals, but I use a variation on ganache which is quicker to make and richer to eat.

FRANZI'S CHOCOLATE ZURISTEI

70 g (2¹/₂ oz) dark chocolate
100 g (3¹/₂ oz) caster sugar
2 tablespoons cocoa powder
150 g (5¹/₂ oz) ground hazelnuts
100 g (3¹/₂ oz) ice-cold unsalted butter, diced
3 eggs
2 tablespoons dark rum
4 sheets of puff pastry

Grate the chocolate and mix in a bowl with the sugar, cocoa and hazelnuts. Add the butter and transfer to a blender. Mix well, then add two of the eggs and the rum. Cover with clingfilm and place in the refrigerator to chill for an hour.

Cut the pastry sheets into circles, about 10 cm (4 inches) in diameter. Place half the circles on buttered baking sheets and brush the edges with the remaining egg, lightly beaten. Place a small spoonful of the chocolate mixture in the middle of each circle and top with another circle of pastry, pressing down at the edges. Brush each one with some of the remaining egg and chill for 15 minutes.

Preheat the oven to Gas Mark 6/200°C/fan oven 180°C.

Bake the pastries for 10 minutes, then lower the heat to Gas Mark 4 /180°C/fan oven 160°C and bake for a further 15 minutes until golden brown.

Makes about 15

Even as an adult I never find the taste disappointing – sweet therapy pure and simple. Whenever I manage to find a bar of Rayon or a packet of those delicious chocolate pebbles, I always think of Franzi and her bulging Merkur bags and long to be back in Schonortli, running into Silvia's room to share them with her.

CHAPTER 10:

Kuchen & Cream

*T*here were women everywhere in Schonortli! We far outnumbered the men and I often felt sorry for Jem, having to amuse himself as the cousins and I ran around with dolls and clothes from our dressing-up box. But despite those women, each of them fighting for their space in the kitchen, kneading pasta dough and making fresh sugo in patterned headscarves to keep the hair off their faces, it was my uncle Corrado who taught me most about food. Like Nonno and my mother, my uncle is a true Italian: passionate, warm, generous, and extremely good looking with deep chocolate-brown eyes and soft olive skin. But perhaps the most obvious thing Corrado has inherited from Nonno is his love of good food and the pride he has always had in sharing it with his family. I always loved watching Corrado at the dinner table at Schonortli, a slice of German *Rhue* bread in one hand and a fork in the other, scraping his plate clean until it shone. It was that healthy gusto, a genuine love of good food and a dismissive intolerance of poor-quality ingredients which taught me how to eat well.

I will never forget the meal my husband and I had the first time we visited him at his home in Parma. We were on our honeymoon and had taken two days out from our stay in Venice to see him before travelling on to Verona. He was an excellent and generous host and greeted us with a warm embrace and a huge chunk of Parmigiano Reggiano. Once you have tasted the real Parmigiano from Parma, no alternative will ever seem as good. We ate fresh egg pasta with dishes of home-made pesto and thick ragu which Satu had made that day, and mopped up the sauces with hunks of delicious *pane rustica*. As a tribute to distant relatives, we ate platters of prosciutto and cold meats like the ones we used to enjoy together in Schonortli and we washed it all down with glasses of his friend's home-made prosecco. After lunch, Corrado went for a long siesta, still the best aid to digestion I know, while Silvia and Laura took us into the town centre for ice cream.

I ordered straciatelle – chocolate chip – which I ate with chocolate and almond tuiles. Ice cream is one of those things I have always been slightly wary of making without a machine, but actually it is surprisingly easy and a great treat for hot sunny days.

STRACCIATELLE ICE CREAM –
TO EAT ON HOLIDAY

500 ml (18 fl oz) full-cream milk
900 ml (1½ pints) single cream
1 vanilla pod, split lengthways
9 egg yolks
200 g (7 oz) caster sugar
200 g (7 oz) dark couverture,
    roughly chopped into small chips

Combine the milk, cream and vanilla pod in a heavy-bottomed pan and bring to the boil.

Whisk the egg yolks and sugar until light and fluffy and gradually pour into the creamy mixture. Reduce the heat to a low simmer and stir constantly until the custard thickens enough to coat the back of a wooden spoon. Remove the vanilla pod and strain the custard into a bowl.

Add the chocolate chips and mix well, then place in a plastic tub and freeze. Check every 10 minutes and stir to avoid crystals forming until the ice cream is firm.

Serves 10

Each year, Corrado drove to Schonortli with Satu and the girls and we often laughed about how the food took up more room in the back than they did. He bought everything straight from the manufacturers so he could be sure of its quality and would bring all sorts of sweet and savoury delicacies he felt we couldn't, or perhaps shouldn't, live without for two weeks. He still visits Switzerland regularly now and my cousin Cristina tells us he does the same thing with Swiss food when he goes back to Parma – loading the car with sweet cooking apples, honey and thick rye bread.

    Silvia and I would always volunteer to go and help him unload the car, running excitedly back to the house with crates of peaches, whole salamis and coppa hams, the obligatory wedge of Parmigiano Reggiano and peccorino cheeses to go with bags of fresh tortellini, and a few bottles of his friend's prosecco. Neither he nor Satu were big drinkers, but they loved a few glasses of the sparkling white wine, and I knew that before long, we would all be sitting down to dinner and raising a glass to cheerful cries of '*Salute*' and '*Cin Cin*'.

One year he brought a special treat for Jem and me – a delicious chocolate log made with nuts and candied fruit and rolled in icing sugar. It looked just like an Italian salami and was so rich we ate only tiny slices of it at a time, although I'm sure Jem quietly scraped away at it while I wasn't looking – just like my aunt Rosalba with Corrina's marzipan carrot when they were girls. It's one of those too-good-to-be-true confections, usually made with golden syrup and black treacle and chilled in a loaf tin. The first time I made it, I was amazed at how easy it was and have since given them away as Christmas presents to sweet-toothed friends.

Salame di Cioccolato

150 g (5½ oz) dark couverture
50 g (1¾ oz) unsalted butter
a pinch of cinnamon
a pinch of ground cloves
100 g (3½ oz) mixed nuts, chopped
50 g (1¾ oz) crushed amaretti biscuits
50 g (1¾ oz) chopped hazelnuts
125 g (4½ oz) mixed dried fruit
icing sugar for coating

Melt the chocolate and butter with the spices in a bain-marie and mix in all the remaining ingredients. Roll into a ball and cover with clingfilm. Chill in the refrigerator for at least 4 hours.

Remove, and mould into a fat sausage. Coat in icing sugar and serve cut into slices with a granita di caffè.

Makes 15–20 slices

Fortunately, Schonortli had a huge, rambling *cantina* for Corrado to put everything in – a cellar which ran the length of the house and was always well stocked with flour for cakes and tarts, risotto rice and delicious fresh fruit. If I hadn't been quite so frightened of it, I'm sure that cellar would have made the perfect hiding place for our games of Murder in the Dark. The walls were made of rough stone and were always cold, even in the height of summer, and there was a maze of dark little passageways, each leading to its own storing chamber. Some of them were blocked off with metal grates and a big padlock, which I always imagined might have been some form of gruesome dungeon in a former life. I can still remember the smell of peaches and cooking apples which hit you as you went in, and the comforting sight of Nonna's green gardening gloves hanging from a hook by the door.

The first night of our Schonortli holidays was always the best and instead of sitting down to a formal dinner in the dining room, we ate Hernli in the hub of the house – the kitchen. At Schonortli, the kitchen was where we prepared our meals and picnics, but unless we were having an afternoon *merenda*, we usually ate in the dining room. So to eat our Hernli in there on the first night was a rare and intimate treat. When we had finished, Nonna would ask Silvia and me to run to the *cantina* to fetch some fruit for dessert. '*Dai, Isabel, prendi una pesca,*' Silvia would say, urging me to try one of the big juicy peaches Corrado had brought. It was always my first peach of the summer as we hardly ever bought them back home, and it tasted like manna from heaven. I would run back down the corridor with her, the sweet sticky juice dripping down my chin.

There were always far more peaches in the *cantina* than any of us could eat and my mother and Satu sometimes turned the ripest ones into jam. I remember one time they added some melted chocolate to the pot, and spread it hot on a slice of bread for each of us children as a special treat. As with many flavours, chocolate complements the taste of fresh peaches perfectly and this delicious spread always reminds me of that succulent fruit in Schonortli. It is lovely on toast, or try using a thin layer of it on top of my Nonna's Napoleon's Torte, before applying the chocolate glaze.

'LEFT-OVERS'
PEACH & CHOCOLATE MERENDA SPREAD

   about 1 kg (2 lb 4 oz) ripe firm peaches
   juice and zest of 1 orange
   juice and zest of 1 lemon
   700 g (1 lb 9 oz) jam sugar
   a pinch of cinnamon
   1 vanilla pod, split lengthways
   300 g (10½ oz) dark couverture, chopped

Peel and quarter the peaches and put with the citrus zest to soak in the citrus juices.

Melt the sugar with the cinnamon in a heavy-bottomed pan, then add the vanilla and leave to infuse.

After about 30 minutes, add the peaches and mix well. Heat again until the jam begins to simmer then remove from the heat and add the chocolate. Mix until all the chocolate has melted. Chill in the refrigerator overnight.

Next day, bring the jam to the boil and heat for about 40 minutes, stirring occasionally. Pour into warm preserving jars, cover with wax paper circles and store for 2–3 weeks in the fridge or eat straight away on warm baguettes.

Makes about 675 g (1½ lb)

Once we had helped clear the dishes, my mother would go for a walk down to the linden trees with Nonna and Nonno, and Corrado and Satu would retire to the *salotto*, leaving us children to play in the *Spielzimmer* with many of the same toys that our parents had had. There were card games and big wooden puzzles and a lovely dressing-up box with long silk gloves and high heels from when Nonna was young. But my favourite thing was my mother's doll's pram. It was a huge ungainly contraption with big rusting wheels and a midnight blue sun-cover. I still have pictures of her pushing it in the garden, a white serviette tied around her head to make her look like a proper nanny. Silvia, the cousin who was closest to me in age, would go and fetch the china doll with its Victorian bonnet and white frilly Communion dress, and we would take it in turns to wheel it through the house.

Dressing-up at Schnortli. Back row, left to right: Cristina, Jem, Laura. Front row, left to right: Silvia, me

Meanwhile, Laura, who was two years older than me, would take charge of closing the green wooden shutters to keep out the *zanzare* – huge mosquitoes which seemed always to make for my mother and myself – and Cristina, the eldest, would remind Jem how to use the Pianola. She would put her feet on the pedals and turn the music pages with self-important gusto, pretending she was actually playing the tunes instead of simply letting herself be guided by the old mechanical contraption.

My aunt Satu was a music teacher at the university in Parma and an excellent violinist. As the granddaughter of the famous Finnish composer Sibelius, she had a rich musical tradition in her own family which she passed on to our cousins. Over the years, she gradually turned the *Spielzimmer* into her study, practising in there most mornings and filling the toy cupboards with her sheet-music. But back then, when we were all little, it was ours, a place where we could play uninterrupted.

But back then, when we were all little, it was ours, a place where we could play uninterrupted

The little wooden table in the centre of the room had a drawer which was always filled with scrap paper and crayons, and the walls were lined with our pictures. Each year we added to the gallery and the last time I went there, when I was nearly 20, I spent almost an entire afternoon looking at them all. Schonortli worked its magic on me again that day and I imagined I could hear the sound of our laughter echoing through the corridors.

By the time the others got back from their walk, it would be pitch black outside and we would gather in the *salotto* for a game before bed. It was Silvia's role to go to the kitchen and prepare a snack of Weihnachtsgebacke – Christmas spice biscuits – and cocoa while the rest of us separated off into groups. Those honeyed gingerbread biscuits came in little star and moon shapes and were coated in hard chocolate icing. I loved them then and still think of them now every time I sit down to a game with my family. They are a little time-consuming to make but extremely rewarding, and delicious with a tall glass of cold milk or some mulled apple juice.

CHOCOLATE-COATED WEIHNACHTSGEBACKE

350 g (12 oz) clear honey
125 g (4½ oz) caster sugar
25 g (1 oz) unsalted butter
400 g (14 oz) plain flour
1 teaspoon ground cinnamon
½ teaspoon grated nutmeg
½ teaspoon ground coriander
½ teaspoon ground cloves
125 g (4½ oz) blanched almonds
50 g (1¾ oz) candied peel
¼ teaspoon cream of tartar
1 tablespoon milk
1 egg, beaten
dark and milk chocolate for icing

Melt the honey, sugar and butter in a heavy-bottomed pan, then sift in the flour and spices.

Coarsely chop the nuts and add to the mixture with the candied peel.

Dissolve the cream of tartar in the milk and stir into the beaten egg, then slowly add them to the mixture. Mix everything together to form a firm dough and place in the refrigerator to cool overnight.

Preheat the oven to Gas Mark 4/180°C/fan oven 160°C.

Roll out the dough to 5 mm (¼ inch) thick and mould into shapes, about 2.5 cm (1 inch) across. Bake for 15 minutes, then leave to cool.

When cool, melt the chocolate and pour on top of the biscuits. (Sometimes, instead of making Omama's name biscuits at Christmas, I make these and cover them in white chocolate then pipe dark chocolate letters on top.)

Makes about 35

CHOCOLAT SUCHARD

By the time Silvia returned, Corrado and Cristina would be setting up the chess set on the table in the far corner of the room, under my father's favourite painting – a ship on stormy waters by Ferdinand Hodler, which was set in an elaborate gilt frame and used to get envious glances from our many visitors. Corrado was a maths professor at the university in Parma and loved to play chess on holiday as he claimed it helped keep his mind sharp. He was extremely good at it, regularly challenging locals on the famous outsized set in the Marktplatz in Berne and is still the undisputed champion in our family.

We all loved the game but secretly crossed our fingers under the table in the hope that we wouldn't be teamed with Nonno, who turned a worrying shade of crimson each time his partner gave a scopa to the other team

Meanwhile, Nonno would be hunting for people to join him in a game of *scopa*. This skilful Italian card game is played in pairs and the idea is to avoid leaving enough cards on the table for your opponents to pick up – clearing the deck and winning themselves a *scopa*. We all loved the game but secretly crossed our fingers under the table in the hope that we wouldn't be teamed with Nonno, who turned a worrying shade of crimson each time his partner gave a *scopa* to the other team.

But my favourite was a Swiss card game called *Schwartz Peter*. Everyone gets dealt a picture card until there are none left. The idea is to find the matching pairs and put them in front of you, offering your hand to the person next to you to pick one from. The only card which doesn't have a match is the *Schwartz Peter*, a chimneysweep who, in our version, was a black cat with a top hat and tails. If you were left holding him in your hand at the end, you had to paint an unsightly black moustache on your face. We used to burn the end of a cork and use that for the forfeit.

When we weren't playing games or chatting, Nonna and Nonno would get out the old projector and we would settle down for a slide show. My mother and Satu would lay out dishes of Kuchen to eat while we watched, with a little jug of fresh Alpine cream to pour on top. These light fruit tarts are a speciality in Switzerland and are usually made with apricots, plums or apples and served to the stallholders on market day in Berne. The marketplace in the centre of the city is surrounded with restaurants called *Kuechliwirtschaft* which specialise in them, and we always used to go for a slice when we were there. You can buy the *Kuchenteig* – the sweet shortcrust pastry dough for the base – at the baker's, which made them a quick and easy way to feed hungry little mouths, and my cousins and I used to eat them at almost every meal in Schonortli. We often used peaches, or apples from the orchard down by the linden, which my mother sliced very thinly and sprinkled with sugar to make them crisp up in the oven.

You can't buy the Kuchenteig in England, so instead she used her trusty shortcrust recipe, which is written on squared paper and stuck to the inside of her kitchen store cupboard

Each night, my father would phone to see how our day had been and I always told him about the Kuchen we had had that day. He is a great lover of fruit tarts and used to make my mother promise to make him one when she got home. You can't buy the *Kuchenteig* in England, so instead she used her trusty shortcrust recipe, which is written on squared paper and stuck to the inside of her kitchen store cupboard. It never fails and I use it now for all my tarts, adding salt instead of sugar for savoury dishes. We had a little greengage tree in our garden at home and she would make one with those and some golden plums and put cocoa powder in the pastry dough. We loved them every bit as much as the ones we ate in Schonortli and always pleaded with her to make some chocolate sauce to go on top.

GOLDEN PLUM KUCHEN
WITH DARK CHOCOLATE SAUCE

about 1 kg (2 lb 4 oz) ripe golden plums
juice of 1 lemon
30 g (1¼ oz) golden caster sugar plus extra
    for sprinkling
For the shortcrust pastry
220 g (7½ oz) plain flour
155 g (5½ oz) ice-cold unsalted butter,
    cut into small cubes
1 egg yolk
5 tablespoons icing sugar
For the chocolate sauce
150 g (5½ oz) dark cooking chocolate
120 ml (4 fl oz) double cream
25 g (1 oz) unsalted butter

Sift the flour into a bowl and add the butter. Blend rapidly until it resembles fine breadcrumbs.

Add 4 tablespoons of cold water to the egg yolk and whisk gently, then add to the flour mixture. Finally, sift in the icing sugar and mix well. Knead the dough for 10 minutes, then roll it into a ball and cover with clingfilm. Chill in the refrigerator for at least 30 minutes.

Meanwhile, prepare the fruit. Stone and thinly slice the plums and toss in a bowl with the caster sugar and lemon juice.

Preheat the oven to Gas Mark 4/180°C/fan oven 160°C.

Take the chilled dough from the fridge and roll out on a floured work surface. Try to get it as thin as you can as the whole point of these tarts is to taste the fruit, not the pastry. Line a buttered 28-cm (11-inch) flan dish with the pastry and arrange the fruit decoratively on top. Sprinkle with a generous helping of golden caster sugar and bake for 15–20 minutes, or until the fruit has slightly caramelised at the edges.

To make the sauce, simply melt the chocolate and cream together in a bain-marie, stirring in the butter at the last minute to give it a glossy finish.

Serves 6 generously

Our slide shows were always a bit of an event at Schonortli, with one of us being put in charge of dimming the lights while the others organised enough chairs for everyone. Nonno would talk us through each slide and Nonna became very territorial over her projector, refusing to let Corrado or my mother intervene even when the pictures started going the wrong way. Both of them had worked so hard all their lives, it was a joy to see those shots of them relaxing on a well-earned cruise down the Nile or on safari in Africa, always dressed in their Agatha Christie-style jodhpurs and white linen shirts. But my favourite films were the old Super-8s: black and white reels of footage of my mother and her family when they were younger. On some of the earlier films we could see my mother's cousins, Hildi and Franzi, skipping down to the pool to play, and her tante Greti and uncle Paul. I loved looking at them all: my relatives, some of whom I hardly knew. There is one film which stands out from the rest in my mind – an image of my mother when she was in her twenties, waving goodbye to Corrado as he left home for his first day at university. She was already working for Marucelli and is wearing a navy blue Chanel-style suit. Standing outside Nonna and Nonno's apartment in Milan, smiling for the camera, she looks more beautiful than I've ever seen her and I still get a welling sense of pride when I think of it.

CHAPTER 11:

Lanterns to the Linden

*W*hen families are spread out, as we were, it is traditions which bind you all together. Schonortli was the place where we could bring those traditions to life and sometimes create new ones too, by being together and living out part of our childhoods under one roof. August 1 was one such occasion. It is a national holiday in Switzerland, dating back to William Tell and the time when the country was given its independence from Austria. The Swiss are a fiercely independent nation to this day and love to celebrate their great moment in history with firework displays, lantern processions and traditional cheese fondues. As children, we all loved the festival, which we spent the entire day preparing for. Jem and I would help our cousins decorate the pine trees in the garden with spiced oranges. We would stick cloves into the skins and hung the oranges from the branches with twine, just like at Christmas, releasing a delicious festive perfume.

*Omama with my
mother and Corrado
at Schonortli, the
terrace decorated for
1 August*

In the early evening Corrado would sound the gong and we all gathered in the dining room for our fondue, but the real festivities began after dark, when we would light our colourful paper lanterns and walk down to the linden trees together. When my mother was little, everyone carried a lantern with the Swiss flag on it, hanging from the end of a long stick, but we would sometimes have brightly coloured flags too, and if I screwed up my eyes and looked long enough, I could see other little lantern processions in the distance, like brightly coloured snakes weaving their way through the hills.

Those displays were spectacular, magical events for children, and I would sit mesmerised

The views of the lake from the linden trees were breathtaking and we would huddle together, wrapped up warmly in thick jumpers and hats, waiting for the fireworks to start. We heard them before we saw them – an impressive booming sound which always had us fooled that it was thunder. It rumbled over the lake, erupting into a riot of colour. Those displays were spectacular, magical events for children, and I would sit mesmerised, watching the giant Catherine wheels and rockets which exploded into hundreds of coloured stars, imagining I was drifting in space with them.

When we got back to Schonortli, we would gather in the *salotto* for toffee apples and pieces of chocolate croccante, or warm slices of my mother's pain d'épices. I loved those evenings, when the cold air made your breath freeze in front of you and the warm sweet food filled you with an almost wintry glow. I always make toffee apples and spice bread on Bonfire Night at home, when the air really is icy, and we have chocolate crocccante inside afterwards as we warm our feet by a roaring fire. Croccante is one of those sweets which is so simple to make you almost don't need a recipe at all. You can use pretty much any hard nut, but almonds and hazelnuts work best for coating in chocolate afterwards.

CHOCOLATE-COATED CROCCANTE – FOR MOCK-WINTER NIGHTS

200 g (7 oz) mixed whole nuts
6 tablespoons caster sugar
100 g (3½ oz) milk chocolate

Scatter the nuts on to a sheet of greaseproof paper, then dissolve the sugar in a heavy-bottomed pan until it is clear and completely melted. Spoon teaspoons of the caramel over little clusters of the nuts and leave to set.

When the croccante has cooled, break it into small, rough pieces.

Melt and temper the chocolate (page 241). Dip the bottom of each piece of croccante into the chocolate just long enough to coat it so that no nuts are showing through. Leave them chocolate side up on a baking tray to set.

Those long, dark evenings were magical times and we would chatter excitedly until late, trying to decide which firework had been the best and who had lost the most pieces of bread in the fondue. Sometimes our cousins would join Satu in playing us some music – Laura on the flute, Silvia on the piano and Cristina on the cello, all looking to their mother for guidance.

On rainy days, when there was nothing to do but play in the *Spielzimmer* or out in the *Haxihus*, Nonna would busy herself with errands and it wasn't uncommon for the cousins to go the entire day without seeing her at all. But on fine, sunny days, she was always up early, rousing the troops in preparation for a good mountain walk. Like my mother, she had been an excellent skier in her youth, but when I was a girl, she preferred to appreciate the mountains where she grew up at a more leisurely pace. An elegant lady, like Omama, Nonna liked to dress well and most days she would wear a smart skirt and blouse or a trouser suit with high heels to match. But in the mountains, dressed down in her walking boots and casual shirt and trousers, she was at her most serene and, to my mind, her most beautiful.

There was an intangible quality to those sunny August mornings, which somehow made you wake earlier than usual – a nervous Christmas-morning excitement welling in the pit of your stomach. The silence over the lake was hypnotic and the early morning air had an icy crispness to it you could almost taste. I loved that quiet time and used to draw it out as long as I could, watching the mountains and drinking in the drama.

We did so many walks on those holidays: short ones when we were all little, where we took the cable car or Alpine trains up to the top and skipped down, and longer, more physically demanding ones when we were older and more

confident walkers. The longest one I have ever done was up to the *Nussbaum*, the nut tree at the top of a steep, steep hill which led on to Schwanden, from where we had the most glorious views of the Eiger, Monch and Jungfrau. One year we all went by cable car up to the Stockhorn and then walked back down to the valley, enjoying an orange sorbet and a slice of Sachertorte when we got there.

The family on a mountain walk. Left to right: Nonna, Silvia, my mother, me, Jem

Nonna and Nonno looked forward to spending the time with us, and our parents took advantage of the occasion to prepare a good hearty picnic. Needless to say, those delicious food parcels were the highlight of my day. Each of us children had different coloured rucksacks in which to carry part of the load; I found mine recently, a little blue one which was so small and compact I am surprised I could fit so much inside.

There would always be enough hard-boiled eggs for one each, which we ate with little individual parcels of salt made with wax paper and some string, a tradition which had started when Nonna was a girl and which my mother would do at home whenever we went fruit-picking with our friends. Sometimes my mother went

down to the baker's in Oberhofen for Weggli, plaited egg-glazed rolls, which Silvia and I filled with Emmenthal and salad, and Cristina and Jem would carry paper parcels of Wurstel to roast on a camp fire. Nonna packed a thermos flask of lemon tea which we would cool in the brook when we were ready to eat and my mother would prepare her delicious Banana Surprise for dessert – small foil-paper parcels of fruit with a few pieces of Lindt chocolate, a little brown sugar and a drizzle of thick Swiss honey, which we roasted on the fire and ate piping hot.

We always took enough food for everyone but that didn't stop us gathering some extra snacks along the way. Satu took us mushroom-picking in the shady mountain passes and Corrado made us all stop for fresh milk, cream and cheese at the many hospitable farmhouses on the hillside terraces. We sometimes came away with more food than we had left home with but had still always worked up enough of an appetite for tea.

Nonna and Nonno enjoyed buying us all a cake when we got down to the valleys. The tearooms were a lovely sight: tiny picture-book chalets with trellised balconies, serving the best post-walk treats Jem and I had ever tasted. My favourites were chocolate sorbets served in hollowed-out orange halves with a few wafer cigars on the side. These are perfect for children, who never tire of the novel presentation, and you can freeze the orange halves for future use. I make the sorbet with some almond essence because it reminds me a little of the Swiss marzipan I love so much.

CHOCOLATE SORBET IN ORANGE CASES

1 cup of strong hot chocolate, cooled
120 g (4½ oz) soft brown sugar
50 g (1¾ oz) dark couverture
2 tablespoons Grand Marnier (optional)
a drop of almond essence
6 hollowed-out orange halves, frozen

Place the chocolate drink, sugar and couverture in a saucepan and heat gently until the ingredients have dissolved. Bring to the boil, then remove from the heat and add about 500 ml (18 fl oz) water, the Grand Marnier, if using, and the almond essence. Mix well.

Freeze the sorbet in a plastic container, stirring every 10 minutes to avoid crystals forming. Transfer to the orange halves while the sorbet is still soft enough to mould into the skins and freeze until firm. Store in the freezer until needed.

Serves 6

By the time we got home it was dark and we were tired, our energy sapped from a day of walking in the crisp mountain air. Satu would make us all crostini with the little mushrooms we had picked lightly sautéd in some cream and tarragon, and we went to bed early, dreaming, no doubt, of what adventures the next day might bring.

As the summer progresses in Switzerland, there is a wonderful sense of drama, with frequent thunderous electric storms breaking the oppressive heat of the day and raging winds making monsters of the pine trees at night. I sometimes lay in my little wooden bed, clutching the duvet up to my nose, listening to the eerie whooshing sound through the trees and enjoying the comfort of being warm, inside. Our rooms were all in a row, so there was safety in numbers, and there was also the sound of the little furry creatures, martens, which had somehow become trapped between the walls and scurried noisily through the house, letting you know that you were never quite alone. Schonortli was a big old house and could have easily seemed cold and frightening to a small child. But it was too loved and lived-in for that and I was never plagued by

A marten

night-time fears while I was there. There were too many people around me to feel scared and too many exciting things to exhaust us during the day.

The only down side of having such a big family, was that Jem and I often didn't have as much time to spend just with Nonna and Nonno as we would have liked. So it was always a special treat when they offered to take us out on our own. I remember those occasions with great fondness and am grateful for them now, as memories I can treasure for ever.

I remember those occasions with great fondness and am grateful for them now, as memories I can treasure for ever

Schonortli was a homely sort of place, where we spent most of our time running around in bare feet, a pair of old jeans and a loose-fitting jumper, but when Nonna and Nonno offered to take us out for the day, we knew we would have to dress up smartly in our Sunday best. Both Jem and I would always pack a special outfit for just such an occasion and I remember spending ages making sure mine was neatly ironed and fresh looking.

Sometimes they would take us up into the mountains for lunch and a walk, other times we were allowed to go on a boat trip and stop somewhere nice for tea. But my favourite days out were the ones we spent in Berne. The picturesque historic city is one of the

*Cristina with
a marten*

prettiest, most sophisticated places I have ever been to. The pavements are wide and immaculately clean, lined with designer clothes shops, jewellers, perfumeries and lovely old tearooms, and the 'rows', covered walkways, give it a unique character as well as protecting shoppers from the frequent downpours. The Marktplatz in the centre of the city has a huge clock tower which chimes the hour with mechanical figures. Designed by Caspar Brunner in 1530, the Zytglogge, as it is known, has a procession of bears, a disgruntled cook and a dancing jester, all coming out to excited cheers from the children who, like Jem and me, had been brought by their grandparents to see it.

I loved looking at all the window displays of the tearooms and patisseries, which always looked mouth-wateringly good

I loved looking at all the window displays, mannequins in exquisite cashmere coats and elegant suits, and of course the tearooms and patisseries, which always looked mouth wateringly good. But of all the shops, our favourite was the toyshop Franz-Karl Weber – an enchanting place on two levels with a winding wooden slide taking you down to the ground floor. We often spent a whole morning in there, and whenever we went with our cousins we would all make a bee-line for the Barbie dolls and sit playing on the floor, as though we were back in our *Spielzimmer* in Schonortli.

My mother stills speaks fondly of her day-trips with Omama when she was a girl, strolling along the rows together and stopping in one of her favourite tearooms before heading home. Nonna used to say she didn't have time for such extravagances, but she made an exception for us – taking Jem and me to Merkur for chocolate and then on for a slice of cake.

The tearooms in Berne were all fabulous, but our favourite place to go for cake was a traditional little patisserie in Interlaken called Schuh. It was on the lake and had an old-fashioned style to it which always made me feel very elegant and privileged. There was a pianist who sat outside in summer and the tables were dressed with crisp white tablecloths and silver cutlery. But the main attraction was the desserts. They were in a glass cabinet inside, and Jem and I always chose the same things: Garak for me, the same little chocolate ganache tart with green icing that my mother used to love as a girl; and a lemon one called Citroen for Jem. They were both about the size of a teacup and were meltingly light with a soft creamy sweetness which was so good it made you smile. I was too young to enjoy tea normally, but here it was different – it was served in painted ceramic cups, and the milk pots were made of chocolate. I always ran inside for more, claiming, unconvincingly I'm sure, that I liked my tea weak.

By the end of our holiday in Schonortli, Jem and I always had a healthy glow to our cheeks, a head full of new Italian words that our cousins had taught us, and enough happy memories to tide us over until the following year. The holidays were over and everyone was going home to work and school, but there was a great comfort in knowing we would all be back again next summer.

Nonna sold Schonortli after Nonno died, and now that it no longer belongs to us, I think of it more than ever – sometimes imagining I can smell the cherry blossom from our tree in the garden or the milk from Frau Amstutz's farm. I feel a deep sadness that I will never be able to walk to the linden with Silvia again, or play in the *Spielzimmer* with Laura, Cristina and Maria Isabella. But the traditions which made those times special live on every time my mother makes one of our favourite chocolate recipes, especially her famous chocolate sandwiches.

CHAPTER 12:

Chocolate Sandwiches

Stories were a common theme which ran through my childhood, the thread which bound us all together and made distant loved ones seem closer. My mother loved telling them while Jem and I loved to listen, wide-eyed with wonder and ready to believe every word, and best of all were the stories she told when she made her chocolate sandwiches. These delectable teatime treats are becoming quite fashionable again, and I hope my children love them as much when they are older as I did then.

My mother's chocolate sandwiches – with their bitter-sweet taste and beautiful decadence – provided a different sort of comfort from the chocolate recipes that passed on culinary traditions and brought us closer as a family. Instead of giving us new family memories to enjoy, they taught us about old ones. They were the tool my mother used to bring our past to life and she usually made them on rainy weekday afternoons, after school, when Jem and I were most in need of a little spirit-lifting. She would always make a plate on the last day of term, a sweet start to our holidays, and years later, when I was home from university for the summer, she made me some and we sat and ate them with a pot of hot chocolate reminiscing about summer holidays with my cousins and grandparents in Switzerland.

We always had a *merenda* when we got in from school, usually a slice of bread and cheese, or a *pain au raisin*, so I suppose chocolate sandwiches were really just an extension of that – a special *merenda* which we enjoyed all the more for knowing we didn't have it that often.

Perched on a kitchen stool, still in my school uniform, I could just about see as my mother cut thin slices of white crusty bread and spread them with butter. She used Menier cooking chocolate for the filling, which came in an emerald green packet with silver foil on the inside and looked like something straight out of one of the German fairy tales she used to tell us in Schonortli. Menier was a little sweeter and thicker than the Lindt bars she used for Nonna's cakes and I loved it, especially when she slipped me a small chunk to suck on while she worked.

These sandwiches are so simple to make they are hardly a recipe at all

These sandwiches are so simple to make they are hardly a recipe at all, but the secret is to use butter cold and hard from the fridge and there is a bit of a knack to spreading it and eating the sandwiches before it melts. The combination of the creamy butter and sweet dark chocolate is a virtually unrivalled pleasure, but if the butter is too warm the whole thing is ruined. My mother used only a few pieces of roughly broken chocolate at a time – so we knew there would be enough for seconds if we were still hungry. If you're making them for your children, always serve with a story and a glass of something warm and spicy. Mulled pear juice is one of my favourites, which I make now with the thick fruit nectar you can buy in most Italian delicatessens, warmed in a pan with a few whole cloves, a slice of orange, a pinch of cinnamon and some lemon zest. Sieve when the mixture is warmed through and serve with a cinnamon stick as a stirrer.

For me, this was chocolate at its best and as a girl I always felt there was something grown-up and mysterious about those little Menier nuggets, which always seemed to take an age to melt in my mouth. We would sit at the kitchen table, Jem and I, quiet and content, as my mother told us about the time our grandpa travelled all the way from Poland to London with his little brothers and sisters in tow, or how Omama used to make home-made doughnuts, called Ringli, to eat with hot drinking chocolate after Midnight Mass on Christmas Eve.

Those stories, just like her cooking, were a sweet tempting mixture of love and nostalgia and they were always far better than any of the ones she read to us from books. She had a way of capturing a mood and creating vivid images in just a few words. She always made sure she told us plenty of stories about our father when he was a boy growing up in the 1920s and 30s with Grandma and Grandpa. I would close my eyes as she spoke and picture him: playing with his little wooden toy cart in the street outside his house, or running off to the Saturday morning matinée at the picture-house with his friends.

My father as a boy (right), in London's East End, 1920s

His mother, my Grandma Jeanie, had grown up in her father's old cinema in the East End and, like my father after her, she loved the drama of those black and white silent films. As soon as she was old enough, she would accompany them on her piano for the audience, making the tunes up on the spot as she watched the images on the screen. My half-sister, Sue, remembers going to Grandma and Grandpa's house for lunch every Saturday, sitting in the big old rocking chair in the kitchen shelling peas, as Grandma told her how she had dreamed of becoming a concert pianist.

Grandma Jeanie put the same energy and passion into her cooking as she did into her playing. Her parents were Russian Jews, immigrants like Grandpa and his family, and just like Nonna and my mother she used food to keep the family traditions and customs alive. My father was an only child, but every Friday night Grandma would invite his cousins and uncles and aunts to supper. One of my favourite stories was about Grandma's Friday night casseroles. London's East End in the early 1920s was a poor but tight-knit community and few women in my father's street had their own oven. Instead, they would all prepare their special Friday night suppers at home the day before and send their children off to the local baker with them to be cooked in his large bread ovens.

My father loved the responsibility and trotted off with his best friend, struggling under the weight of Grandma's huge casserole dish. He says he can still remember the mouthwatering smell of everyone's dinner cooking in those big furnaces and used to wait outside with his friends until they were ready. But despite being proud to help, he also had a mischievous streak and loved to play a little trick. Making sure the baker wasn't watching, he would lift the lid of each of the pots, which all looked fairly similar, and peer inside, looking for the one with the most meat, dumplings and potatoes in it. When he found it, he would carry it home, licking his lips and feeling very pleased with himself. Grandma scolded him each time, but I think she was secretly quite pleased that her little Harry was so enterprising – besides, it gave them a good dinner-table story to tell.

Grandma loved to cook and had a healthy appetite to match, regularly treating my father and Grandpa to good traditional Jewish dishes which had been passed down in her family. But the most important meal she ever cooked was the first one she made for my mother, her future daughter-in-law. No two women will ever be more possessive over a man than a Jewish mother and an Italian wife. Grandma, who cared little for modern trends and fancy cooking, made her famous stuffed neck: the skin of a chicken's neck stuffed with the liver, herbs, spices and breadcrumbs and roasted in its own juices. She decided my mother needed some feeding-up and prepared a banquet of her favourite dishes to go with it: gefilte fish, chopped herring, buttered chalah – all of them delicious, fattening, heart-cloggingly good recipes that she had been brought up on.

To end the meal, she made my father's favourite dessert: apple strudel. Anyone who has tasted my grandma's strudel agrees it is the best they have ever had. She made the lightest, flakiest pastry and filled it with almonds, raisins, huge, juicy cooking apples, cinnamon and a secret ingredient which was nevertheless instantly recognisable – chocolate. I don't know how much she put in, but it was always just enough and melted into the pastry to form a dark, sugary crust. Grandma's strudel recipe was a secret for as long as she was alive but Sue now has it and makes it when she's missing her most. My father still smiles with pride when he thinks of it, and insists that despite keen searching on his part he has never found one as good.

GRANDMA'S SECRET CHOCOLATE STRUDEL

125 ml (4 fl oz) full-cream milk
125 g (4½ oz) unsalted butter
100 g (3½ oz) caster sugar
500 g (1 lb 2 oz) self-raising flour
a pinch of cinnamon
3 eggs
icing sugar
For the filling
125 g (4½ oz) sweet chestnut jam
75 g (2¾ oz) dark chocolate, chopped
about 12 Pink Lady apples, peeled and thinly sliced
4 tablespoons vanilla sugar (page 242)
250 g (9 oz) mixed dried fruit
50 g (1¾ oz) blanched almonds, sliced
1 teaspoon mixed spice
½ teaspoon ground cloves
juice of ½ lemon
30 g (1¼ oz) cold unsalted butter, cubed

To make the pastry, melt the milk, butter and sugar in a heavy-bottomed pan over a low heat until the sugar has dissolved. Set aside to cool.

Place the flour and cinnamon in a bowl and make a well in the centre. Add two beaten eggs and the cooled milk mixture and mix to form a soft dough. Knead for 10–15 minutes depending on how strong your arm is. Wrap in clingfilm and chill in the refrigerator for 30 minutes.

Preheat the oven to Gas Mark 4/180°C/fan oven 160°C.

Roll the pastry into a long rectangular sheet about 5 mm (½ inch) thick. Spread the centre third of the pastry with the jam and sprinkle the chocolate over. Toss the apples in the vanilla sugar and add the mixed fruit, nuts and spices and a little lemon juice and spread over the chocolate. Sprinkle with half the butter.

Brush the edges with beaten egg and fold the sides of the pastry rectangle over the apple mixture. Melt the remaining butter and brush over the top of the strudel. Bake for 45 minutes.

When it has cooled, dust with icing sugar and serve with fresh cream.

Serves 8

He would mix his soup, meat, veg, dessert and drink together and wolf it down with such a speed neither she nor Grandpa had time to stop him

My mother loved that meal, and food that day acted as mediator, interpreter and friend to both of them – a confidant they shared and a pleasure they both enjoyed.

My father loved everything his mother made for him, so I was surprised when Grandpa told Jem and me about one of his favourite dinner-table habits as a boy. Being an only child, he made the most of the time he had playing with his friends and he used to beg Grandma to let him put his whole meal in one bowl, so he could eat it quickly and run outside. He would mix his soup, meat, veg, dessert and drink together and wolf it down with such a speed neither she nor Grandpa had time to stop him – Harry's Polish soup they used to call it, a brave concoction.

For me, Grandpa bridged that gap between the past and the present and I used to beg my mother to repeat the story of how he came over from Poland in the late 1890s, a boy of 12 with the weight of the world on his shoulders. I must have been no older than five or six when she first told me about the boat journey over from his home near Warsaw. His mother, who had been too ill to travel, dreamed of a better life for her little children and sent them to England to stay with an uncle.

No one is quite sure now how many of them there were on that trip, all we know is that Grandpa was one of 10 children and had to grow up pretty fast. As the oldest, he had been trusted with the fare money, which he kept in the pocket of his shorts. He badly wanted to prove how responsible he was, but rather over-awed at the prospect of leaving his home and parents for a new life abroad, he lost the precious money before he had even boarded the ship. Desperate not to let his poor mother down, he came up with a plan: he would sell lemons to the other passengers on the boat, telling them they would cure their seasickness. Luckily, it worked and he made enough money for the tickets and a little extra for lunch.

Starting a new life in London was a daunting prospect for a poor Polish boy who barely spoke enough English to say his own name. But Grandpa was a true survivor and before long he had found work as an apprentice tailor, a trade which he would practise until he was well into his eighties. Years later, when my father was a boy, Grandpa worked as an outside tailor for Harrods. My father tells me with a mischievous glint in his eye that as Grandpa sewed hems for the models at the kitchen table, he would sit on the floor underneath, peering up their skirts.

Grandpa was excellent at what he did and would often sew the buttons back on to my school uniform for me when I was little. My father respected his skill so much that each time he was offered a design post, he insisted the company employ Grandpa along with him.

When I was a child, Grandpa seemed ancient to me. No one really knew for sure how old he was, since he had lost his birth certificate along with his money on that eventful boat trip. But from the stories he told me, I guessed he must have been at least 95 when he died, almost 20 years ago. He once described to Jem and me how he had waved to Queen Victoria as she rode through London in a horse-drawn coach, just as Omama had done, and that he remembered seeing Oswald Mosley march through the streets of London years later, when my father was a teenager – an alarming sight for a young Jewish immigrant.

Of all those stories, the most poignant for me was the one about Uncle Harry. Grandpa had so many siblings and cousins that it was virtually impossible to keep tabs on them all, but Uncle Harry was Grandma's brother. He can't have been much older than 17 or 18 when he was sent to the trenches during the First World War, and he used to write regular letters home to Grandpa and Grandma, who was by then pregnant with my father. My father still has a birthday card that Harry sent Grandma – a decorative postcard with the message: 'May you have many friends and no foes' written on the back.

In his letters he wrote of how he longed to come home and see them and the new baby, who Grandma and Grandpa named after him. Tragically, the two Harries would never meet and shortly afterwards, Uncle Harry was killed at the front line. But those letters live on, and whenever my father is

In his letters he wrote of how he longed to come home and see them and the new baby, who Grandma and Grandpa named after him

missing his family, he gets them out, along with an old sepia photograph of the teenager he never knew. The sight of that gentle, innocent face still brings a tear to his eye, and to mine when he tells me about it.

My childhood was enriched with these stories and I will always be grateful to my mother for telling them to me, just as I am for her wonderful home cooking. Whether she was turning popping corn black with grated chocolate and spoonfuls of honey, or risotto rice golden with a few saffron strands and some vermouth, I always felt she had performed some sort of unspoken magic.

There was a wonderful sense of creativity in our home when I was growing up, which I attribute to my parents' love of art and their youthful sense of adventure. It seemed to me that everything they did fuelled my imagination and gave me the passion for life I have today, and I still believe my love of cooking and good food stemmed from that time. At Christmas, we would make popcorn decorations together, stringing the pieces on to a length of coloured twine and hanging them from the beams in our hallway. My mother taught me to bake spiced gingerbread biscuits for decorating the tree and how to make potato prints for Christmas cards. Together we mixed flour with oil and water and added food colouring to make play dough and used it to create huge batches of fake marzipan fruits.

Making play dough is one of those seemingly simple pastimes, and incredibly rewarding. The best part is knowing that if your inquisitive little toddler decides to eat it, it won't do them any harm. My mother used to let me use her kitchen utensils to sculpt with afterwards and I especially loved crushing it with her meat tenderiser and then shaping it with her biscuit cutters.

FOOD-COLOURING PLAY DOUGH –
FOR CREATIVE TOTS

500 g (1 lb 2 oz) plain flour
125 g (4½ oz) salt
2 teaspoons cream of tartar
2 teaspoons sunflower oil
food colouring

Combine the flour, salt and cream of tartar and make a well in the centre as you would if you were making pasta dough. Pour 250 ml (9 fl oz) water and the oil into the centre and mix well, kneading with a strong arm for several minutes until it's glossy and firm.

Separate the mixture into small balls and add a few drops of different food colouring to each one.

To store it, wrap in clingfilm and place in a plastic container in a cool place.

The last time I ate chocolate sandwiches with my mother, I was pregnant with my daughter. I had just got over my morning-sickness and craved them more than ever – desperate for something that wasn't toast or dried crackers. We sat at the kitchen table together, as we always used to, and went through the photo albums of us all in Schonortli that my aunt Corrina had sent after Nonna died. It was a strange and poignant time, awaiting a birth and mourning a death, thinking of the family more than ever and wondering what would have happened if we hadn't sold Schonortli. Our conclusion was that we didn't need it any more, we had learnt the lesson it was supposed to teach us: that family is the most important thing in the world; and we vowed that we would eat chocolate sandwiches together for many years to come.

CHAPTER 13:

All about My Mother

s a little girl, I loved to watch my mother cook and I remember I could tell what mood she was in by the food she made. When she was sad and missing Italy, she would make fresh pasta, showing me how to feed it through the pasta machine and dry it over the back of a kitchen chair. When we got back from Schonortli and her homesickness was at its worst, she would make potato gnocchi, rolling the little balls with a fork to make shell-like shapes and preparing her famous home-made tomato sugo to go with them. And when she was happy, she liked to experiment, making fruit and nut tarts with almond pastry, meringues with pine nuts and chocolate cream fillings, and the most delicious chocolate soufflés imaginable.

Sitting down at the kitchen table, a cup of chocolate and a biscuit in front of her, she would look through her recipes, deciding what to make. She had two drawers full of tattered old cookery books held together with sellotape and string, cookery cards she had collected from magazines over the years, and recipes she had written down on squared paper from her mother and grandmother. She had kept the notes she made on her cookery course in Milan and had stuck in ideas from the restaurants my father had taken her to before they were married. There seemed to be a never-ending supply of ideas, a tempting mixture of French, Swiss and Italian as well as some traditional English recipes she had gathered to keep my father happy. Most of them were dessert recipes with her own annotations on the side, usually in Italian.

She had two drawers full of tattered old cookery books held together with sellotape and string, cookery cards she had collected from magazines over the years, and recipes she had written down on squared paper from her mother and grandmother

When she wasn't cooking for a dinner party or trying out new dishes for us, she would work on her jewellery or knitting – more of her hobbies, which like everything else she did had become an art form. I must have been about six or seven when she first tried to teach me to knit, just as Omama had done with her. But I didn't take to it, and preferred instead to watch her as she worked. She would knit in the evenings, just before my bedtime, and I would sit curled up next to her, listening to the clink clink clink of her needles and wondering what creation she would end up with.

She made so many beautiful jumpers and cardigans when I was little, as well as dresses and jerkins for me. They were all her own designs with a palette of colours to match her mood, just like her cooking: aubergine and purple when she was feeling dark and missing home; citrus orange and lemon in summer, when the occasional sunshine had lifted her spirits; and rusts, browns and orange in autumn when the fallen leaves and berries in the fields near our home filled her with renewed inspiration. Of all her creations, the one I loved most was a high-necked cardigan she made one summer. Its colour, a subtle, grainy oatmeal pink, reminded me of my favourite dessert – her hazelnut and raspberry meringue. Whenever my mother wore that cardigan, I would beg her to make the cake, which consisted of two large round hazelnut meringues filled with chocolate cream and fresh raspberries. It was irresistibly moreish, chewy on the inside and sugary crisp on the outside, just like the Japonais Omama had treated her to years before in Berne. She has passed the recipe on to me, but I must confess I still can't quite make it taste the way she did when I was a girl. The meringue sandwiches must be slightly gooey in the centre, that way you can mix them into the sweet cream filling for a truly decadent treat.

HAZELNUT MERINGUE CAKE WITH RASPBERRIES & CHOCOLATE CREAM

4 egg whites
250 g (9 oz) caster sugar
100 g (3½ oz) ground hazelnuts
200 ml (7 fl oz) whipping cream
1 tablespoon icing sugar
3 tablespoons cocoa powder
2 punnets of fresh raspberries

Preheat the oven to Gas Mark ½/120°C/fan oven 100°C.

Whisk the egg whites until stiff, then slowly start adding the sugar until you have a firm glossy mixture. Fold in the hazelnuts and divide the meringue mixture between two 20-cm (8-inch) cake tins.

Bake for about 45 minutes, then leave to cool.

Meanwhile, whip the cream with the icing sugar and cocoa powder and fold in the raspberries.

Sandwich the meringues with some of the cream, then use the rest to decorate the top. Dust with icing sugar and serve chilled.

Serves 6–8

For as long as I can remember, my mother has had a project. When I was tiny, it was illustrating her cousin Franzi's first children's book, then, when Jem and I were at school, she took a silversmithing course, and now she is making beautiful hand-embroidered pieces for exhibitions and private collections. Each time, she immerses herself in her work, producing reams of highly skilled preliminary sketches. I used to love watching her paint ideas down for the brooches and earrings she made when I was little, using brown artist's paper and watercolours. I would sit at the kitchen table next to her, drawing or doing my homework, sneaking a look at what she was doing every now and then and hoping I would be as talented as her one day. Sometimes she asked for my opinion, holding up several sketches and telling me to choose the best.

I remember that once she made caramel swirls on a sheet of acetate paper, when she was trying to come up with ideas for a necklace design. She wanted something free and had been trying for hours to find a pattern she liked, when she thought of doing it with sugar. It was fun to watch and even more fun to eat afterwards and she ended up making a very modern silver necklace which sold almost immediately. Making caramel swirls is fun, but if you have small children in the house you will have to keep a keen eye on them as hot sugar can give you the most terrible burns. I sometimes make these when I can't think of a better decoration for a birthday cake. You can add cocoa powder for a richer taste and colour and a little edible gold leaf for a special finish.

Caramel Swirls for Fun & Cakes

150 g (5½ oz) caster sugar
1 heaped tablespoon cocoa powder
1 sheet edible gold leaf for decoration

Simply melt the sugar in a pan on a low heat and simmer gently until it turns a rich golden brown (5–10 minutes). Add the cocoa powder and stir well, then remove from the heat and, using a teaspoon, swirl on to a sheet of lightly buttered greaseproof paper or a well-greased baking tray.

While the sugar is still soft (don't touch it with your finger, test with the back of a spoon), sprinkle tiny bits of edible gold leaf on top. Leave to set then break off with a spatula.

Eat straight away or stick into a gooey chocolate cake or fudge brownie.

Growing up with good food was something I used to take very much for granted, but now that I have children of my own, I realise how important it is to eat well and set them a good example from an early age. Everything my mother made for Jem and me was freshly prepared with good ingredients and when I think back to my favourite meals as a girl, most of them involved some sort of vegetable or fruit. I still phone my mother today, asking her for the ingredients list for her spinach tart or courgettes in the oven, and when I want something quick and healthy I use her recipe for mushroom frittata or minestrone soup. Although cakes and biscuits were an occasional treat, somehow even they tasted healthy.

This was true of one of my favourite teatime cakes – a marble cake she had found in one of Omama's cookery books. Sliced thinly, with a generous drizzle of cream on top, it looked like something from one of the tearooms Omama used to take her to when they were on holiday. She made it for us on many occasions and for years I thought all marble cakes would taste like hers, until one day I tried a shop-bought one and was bitterly disappointed. Hers was always moist and fudgy in the centre and she later confided that the secret to making each of the colours taste of something different was to use home-made flavourings. She used the pulp of a fresh vanilla pod crushed in milk for the white part; ground pistachio nuts for the green; home-made raspberry coulis, which she strained through a fine sieve, for the red; and, of course, melted dark chocolate and bitter cocoa powder for the dark part. It was the most delicious loaf cake I had ever tasted and is worth every second of the time it takes to prepare. I make it very occasionally, when I have an afternoon to myself, and love it slightly warm from the oven with fresh pouring cream drizzled on top.

My Mother's Marble Cake –
FOR TEA WITH THE GIRLS

100 g (3½ oz) dark chocolate
2 tablespoons cocoa powder
125 ml (4 fl oz) full-cream milk
1 vanilla pod, split lengthways
200 g (7 oz) vanilla sugar (page 242) or caster sugar
150 g (5½ oz) unsalted butter, softened
1 teaspoon vanilla extract
2 eggs, beaten
300 g (10½ oz) self-raising flour
1 small punnet of fresh raspberries
juice of 1 lemon
25 g (1 oz) whole pistachio nuts
a little green food colouring
icing sugar

Melt the chocolate, then stir in the cocoa powder and leave to cool. Place the milk in a bowl with the vanilla pod and leave to infuse.

Beat the sugar, butter and vanilla extract in a blender until light and fluffy. Beat in the eggs a little at a time, followed by the vanilla-flavoured milk. Transfer to a mixing bowl and gently stir in the flour.

Crush the raspberries with the lemon juice in a mortar and pestle and pass through a fine sieve.

Preheat the oven to Gas Mark 4/180°C/fan oven 160°C.

Divide the mixture between four bowls. Add the chocolate to the first one, the nuts and colouring to the second, the raspberries to the third and leave the fourth plain.

Drop large spoonfuls of each mixture alternately into a greased and lined 25-cm (10-inch) loaf tin until there is none left. Using a flat-bladed knife, swirl through the mixture gently. Bake for 1 hour.

Dust with icing sugar and serve warm.

When my parents bought their house, nearly 40 years ago, the garden was so wild and overgrown that I once dreamt I saw a tiger weaving in and out of the tall blades of grass! Now, my mother has more time to spend on it – tending to her roses and bougainvillea and the clay flower pots she has dotted around the patio – but when I was little, it was an unordered place, perfect for magic and make-believe. And there was no better time to see that magic come to life than at Easter. My mother used to hard-boil a few eggs in a pan and, when they were cool enough, we would help her paint patterns on them with food colouring. She taught us how to get a marbled effect, and when we were very little we would paint smiley faces on them and eat them with some salt, just like we did on those wonderful picnics at Schonortli.

There was always a hushed buzz of excitement in our house on Easter morning. I remember Jem and I being sent into the lounge to play while my mother closed the kitchen door secretively behind her

There was always a hushed buzz of excitement in our house on Easter morning. I remember Jem and I being sent into the lounge to play while my mother closed the kitchen door secretively behind her. Later that morning, she would call us in. 'I think I saw the Easter bunny in the garden, don't you?' she would say, looking to my father for confirmation. It seemed to take us all morning to find the goodies hidden among the flowers, under bushes, inside our shed and on top of the wooden swing and climbing frame. We each had a little basket for our finds, which we spread out on the lawn when we had finished. There was usually a handful of mini Lindt eggs each, wrapped in green shiny paper, with creamy centres which melted in the mouth. Sometimes we would have a few sugar-shelled mini eggs too and always one big one each. Some years, Franzi sent us a large Swiss Easter bunny which my mother decorated with a bright red ribbon. I remember unwrapping a tiny corner of the purple foil and breaking off a piece of milk chocolate. It seemed sweeter and thicker than any of the eggs I have had since and took me weeks to finish.

After our egg hunt, we all helped decorate the kitchen table with daffodils and buttercups from the garden before sitting down to a traditional Italian lunch of roast lamb with rosemary potatoes. I loved the crisp minty crust my mother made for the meat, but always reminded myself to save enough room for dessert.

Easter is an important festival in Italy and families who have been restrained during Lent look forward to rewarding themselves with a sumptuous feast on Easter day. When my mother was a girl, they used to have Torta Pasqualina, a traditional Ligurian pie made with whole eggs, ham, cheese and greens. I have eaten this as picnic food in Rome where it was made with Fontina and Swiss chard and there is nothing quite like the smell of it in the streets of Italy around Easter, when the bakers' windows are filled with similar festival breads, chocolate eggs and panettone.

My mother loved the savoury pie but, like me, always saved room for dessert. It is traditional to eat a special type of panettone at Easter, called Colomba, which is shaped like a dove and topped with crystallised sugar and flaked almonds. I love it, especially when there is a thin layer of frangipane under the sugar crust. Panettone was one of the few things my mother didn't bother to make herself as no matter how carefully you follow a recipe, the ones you buy in shops are always better. Instead, we often cut slices of Colomba and ate it grilled with a traditional Italian chocolate sauce. Colomba, with its sweet nutty taste, is ideal for this, but you can use ordinary panettone too.

EASTER COLOMBA WITH CHOCOLATE SAUCE

500 ml (18 fl oz) full-cream milk
I vanilla pod or 1 teaspoon vanilla essence
6 large egg yolks
175 g (6 oz) caster sugar
25 g (1 oz) '00' plain cake flour
a pinch of salt
100 g (3½ oz) dark chocolate (70% cocoa solids), grated
1 tablespoon amaretto
several thick slices of Colomba, toasted

Boil the milk in a pan with the vanilla. Beat in the egg yolks, sugar, sifted flour and salt and mix until smooth and creamy. Then add the grated chocolate and stir until melted. Add the amaretto at the end and pour hot over the warmed slices of Colomba.

Eat immediately with a thimble glass of amaretto or brandy.

Serves 8–10

Growing up with Italian, Polish, Swiss and Russian blood in me, the child of a Jewish father and Roman Catholic mother, the one thing which brought us all together was food and the traditions we shared whenever we ate together. Sitting down to Friday night supper with Grandpa felt as natural as eating fondue with Nonna and Nonno on 1 August. I listened to my father say prayers on Seder night and went to church with my mother on Christmas morning, and both Jem and I grew up feeling enriched and enlightened as a result. But birthdays were different. They were one of the few occasions which everyone celebrated in the same way and when we all ate the same things. I was always secretly very proud of my mother's cooking skills and looked forward to my birthday parties as a time when I could show her off to my friends. It started with the cake, which we were always allowed to choose. We could have Nonna's Napoleon's Torte, a rich Sachertorte made with breadcrumbs and almonds for a grainy texture and decorated with chocolate butter icing, chocolate curls on the side and her hand-made chocolate shapes on top. I made this for my husband the first year we were married but remember being disappointed that it didn't taste quite right. I phoned my mother and complained but she soon put me right: I had forgotten the thin layer of apricot jam she always spread before pouring the butter icing on top. Somehow the tanginess of the fruit makes the whole thing that little bit special and counteracts the bitterness of the chocolate icing.

Our other choice was my mother's own special invention. There really isn't a name for this soft creamy concoction that Jem and I loved so much. It was more of an assembly job than a cake, and consisted of two soft cocoa sponges, filled and topped with chocolate mousse and decorated with chocolate sprinkles, marzipan fruits, and our names written in dark chocolate piping. It was utterly divine and if there was ever any left over by the evening, you could be sure the fairies would have eaten it by morning.

My third birthday – with my mother's famous chocolate birthday cake

I must admit, I had a hard time choosing between the two and sometimes even asked for my mother's hazelnut meringue instead, but I think her mousse cake had the slight edge, especially as I now know she put a tiny amount of rum in the creamy filling for an added kick. This is simple to make, and I sometimes cheat and buy the sponges ready-made. Make a large quantity of Omama's Chocolate Mousse and spread it in the middle of the two cakes and all over the outside. Pat chocolate sprinkles around the edges and pipe chocolate cream on top. Serve on paper plates to hungry children and wait for the cries of 'More, please.'

When we were older, Jem and and I were allowed to help my mother make a favourite birthday 'filler' which had the rather undignified title of Pineapple Mess. It was something she came up with one day when she had some leftover chocolate in the mixing bowl after baking our birthday cake and is so simple it really doesn't warrant a formal recipe of its own. All you do is cut thin slices of chocolate cake, top them with half a pineapple ring and a glacé cherry and pour melted milk chocolate over the top. Chill them in the fridge for half an hour and eat as soon as the chocolate has hardened, or before if you really can't wait.

My mother taught me how to have fun with cooking, and my best memories are of watching her in the kitchen. She used to love giving dinner parties when Jem and I were little and I always remember being proud to help as she chopped, marinated and whisked, coming up with innovative and adventurous recipes she loved sharing with her friends. Jem and I were always allowed to sample the meal before her guests arrived. There was always a starter, and my favourite was her marinated Mushrooms à la Grecque which she served in tiny white ramekins with a sprig of fresh parsley. But the desserts were her favourite, another good excuse to try out a new recipe, and she made such a selection of them I still struggle to decide which I liked best. I remember licking the bowl after she had prepared an Italian zabaglione and thinking it was the creamiest, sweetest thing I had ever tasted. In the summer she sometimes made a feather-light raspberry soufflé with a rich plain-chocolate sauce and one time she made a chocolate and hazelnut roulade. This is a favourite of mine and quite simple to prepare, although rolling it without it splitting down the middle can prove quite an art.

MY MOTHER'S BEST CHOCOLATE ROULADE

3 medium eggs
150 g (5½ oz) caster sugar
75 g (2¾ oz) potato flour or arrowroot
2 teaspoons baking powder
2 tablespoons cocoa powder
icing sugar

For the filling
200 ml (7 fl oz) double or whipping cream
1 tablespoon icing sugar
4 tablespoons cocoa powder

Preheat the oven to Gas Mark 4/180°C/fan oven 160°C.

Whisk the eggs and sugar at high speed until thick and mousse-like. Sift the flour with the baking powder and cocoa and cut into the egg mix.

Pour into a greased and lined 20 x 30-cm (8 x 12-inch) Swiss roll tin and bake for 10 minutes. Set aside to cool.

Meanwhile, prepare the filling. Whip the cream, sugar and cocoa powder together until stiff and forming peaks.

Turn the cooled roll on to a lighly sugared sheet of greaseproof paper. Spread with the filling and roll up carefully.

Serve chilled, dusted with icing sugar.

Serves 8

CHAPTER 14:

Christmas Magic & Make-believe

*T*he memories I have of my mother's cooking are precious to me and I hope they never fade. Perhaps the best memories of all are the ones of Christmases at home when I was a girl. Something happened in our home in December which filled the air with mystery and wonder and made anything seem possible. Even today, I get the same childlike excitement from baking Christmas treats as I did when I was little and I hope my children will feel it too one day – the joy of old family recipes at their best.

Children were made for magic. A dish of half-eaten mince pies and an empty sherry glass were all it took to send my brother and I into paroxysms of delight when we were little, running madly through the house shouting to whoever would listen that Father Christmas had been down our chimney.

I have happy memories of sitting at our kitchen table as my mother prepared the cake, writing my Christmas list and dreaming of presents and filled stockings. Suddenly the wardrobes in my parents' room were off-limits and the kitchen cupboards were filled with marzipan, currants and spices, all the things we needed to make our favourite festive delicacies.

It all started on 1 December when Jem and I woke to find Advent calendars pinned to our bedroom doors. They were always traditional ones, shimmering with glitter, showing scenes of woodland animals covered in snow and tinsel and Father Christmas darting off into the distance on his reindeer-driven sleigh. I spent hours looking at the pictures, wondering what was behind each door and willing it to be Christmas Eve so I could open the last one.

School was always winding down by then and lessons were spent learning carols and preparing for the end of term play. I loved the festive buzz in the air and used to come home each day, my head full of myths and legends, eager for my mother to retell the stories I had learnt. She would make a plate of her dark chocolate-coated orange peel, scented with a little nutmeg and cinnamon, to eat as we chatted. I always thought those chocolates looked like little precious jewels, shimmering in the half light of the angel chime Nonna had sent us from Switzerland, dark on the outside and chewy and golden on the inside. When she first told me of the Three Kings and the gold, frankincense and myrrh, I imagined their gifts to look just like that – rich, precious nuggets glowing in the half-light of the moon. I bit into the sweet fruit and listened as she told me about Balthazar, the king of Saba where frankincense flowed from the trees. Coated orange peel is simple sorcery, and I love making it now for my family and friends.

We always knew Christmas was on its way when my mother bought panforte, a sticky, satisfyingly rich cake which we still eat with mulled wine or strong coffee. It is made with nuts, honey and candied fruit and is dense, gooey and tooth-tinglingly good. Part of its charm, for me, is the story of how it originated.

Legend has it that the original *panpepato*, peppered bread from which panforte was later created, was a happy accident which came about in the 1200s in Sienna. Suor Leta, a young nun, was cleaning out the spice cupboards for her Mother Superior when she noticed that the bags of nuts and fruit they had been given as gifts from passing pilgrims had been eaten away by mice and the contents had all spilled out. There was a terrible mess and she decided the best thing would be to throw it all away and clear out the cupboards, but just as she was about to fetch a brush, a black cat crossed her path. It jumped in front of her, and she was sure she heard it say: 'Why not throw it all in a pan and put it on the fire to cook?'

Without thinking, she followed its instructions, adding some sugar and flour and stirring it with a big wooden spoon. The sweet smell was intoxicating and the cat urged her to try the cake. She raised the spoon to her mouth and was about to taste it when she suddenly came to her senses. 'Cats don't speak,' she told herself, 'but the Devil does.' She grabbed the pot and threw the cake over the poor creature's head, fleeing before anyone saw her. But she was overheard by the Mother Superior, who came to see what all the noise was about. Seeing the remains of the honeyed mixture on the floor, she thought it would be a crime to waste all those generous offerings and sat down to the best meal she had ever had. From then on, they made *panpepato* every year and offered it to the passing pilgrims as a Christmas treat.

Chocolate was first added to the recipe in the 1820s and now there are two varieties of panforte: Panforte Nero made with bitter almonds and dark couverture and Panforte Margherita, originally made for Queen Margherita in 1879, with sweet almonds and candied pumpkin.

My mother usually bought our panforte from an Italian shop she knew and laid it on a big white plate with pink ceramic flowers around the edge, ready for Christmas Eve. But some years she made it herself, adding some chocolate for a darker colour and richer flavour. This recipe is a combination of the two types with a lovely aftertaste coming from the sweet almonds and a rich dark colour to the caramel centre. Eat it in thin slices on Christmas Eve as we did, or cut it into small, torrone-sized rectangles and wrap them in decorative paper for a St Nicholas's Day treat. I had heard that this is one of the hardest cakes to make yourself and didn't attempt it for years. But don't be put off, this recipe is a winner and will come out better than the ones you buy in shops as long as you use the secret ingredient – candied pumpkin.

CHRISTMAS PANFORTE NERO

250 g (9 oz) blanched almonds, lightly toasted
125 g (4½ oz) halved walnuts
2 teaspoons ground cinnamon
1½ teaspoons ground coriander
1 teaspoon mixed spice
200 g (7 oz) '00' plain cake flour
2 heaped tablespoons bitter chocolate
     (at least 80% cocoa solids), grated
50 g (1¾ oz) bitter chocolate, in chunks
200 g (7 oz) caster sugar
200 g (7 oz) clear honey
50 g (1¾ oz) mixed candied peel
250 g (9 oz) zucca (candied pumpkin), cubed
grated zest of 1 orange
icing sugar

Preheat the oven to Gas Mark 3/160°C/fan oven 140°C.

Mix the nuts and spices, and add the sifted flour and the chocolate.

Heat the sugar and honey with 1 tablespoon of cold water until dissolved, then increase the heat and stir until it bubbles and forms a pale, thickened caramel. Pour the hot mixture over the nuts and flour and mix quickly before it solidifies too much. Stir in the candied fruits and orange zest and mix well.

Line a 20-cm (8-inch) cake tin with rice paper and pour the mix in. Smooth it down by placing a sheet of foil on top and placing a heavy saucepan over it. Bake for 30 minutes.

Leave to cool, then dust with icing sugar.

Happily, my mother has passed the delightful sweet tradition of St Nicholas's Day on to us. For as long as I can remember, I have been leaving my slipper outside my bedroom door on the night of 5 December, and waking the next morning to find it filled with chocolates, oranges and nuts. As children, Jem and I would always try and get the better of St Nicholas, waiting up until we could hardly keep our eyes open. But somehow he always managed to pass through our home unseen. I can still picture my slipper now, bulging with nuts, ripe tangerines and bags of chocolate coins. There was never enough to make us sick, but always plenty to keep us happy in the long run-up to Christmas.

Making sweets is fun and easy and I must admit I don't usually wait until Christmas to do it. But my favourite St Nicholas's Day fillers are little chocolate-orange almonds wrapped in gold paper, because they are so simple to make and you can fit quite a number even in a small person's slipper.

CHOCOLATE-ORANGE ALMONDS FOR ST NICHOLAS'S DAY

> 200 g (7 oz) dark orange-flavoured chocolate
> 1 teaspoon ground cinnamon
> 200 g (7 oz) whole dry-roasted almonds, skins on
> icing sugar

Temper the chocolate (page 241) in a bain-marie and add the cinnamon.

Dip each almond in the chocolate and leave on a sheet of baking parchment to set.

When they have cooled, dust them with icing sugar and wrap in gold paper.

Leave a few in a little slipper with a tangerine and some whole walnuts.

We spent ages each year decorating our fireplace at home with mistletoe and cards to give the room an inviting glow. My mother had a little nativity scene, *il presipino*, which she had had as a child and we set it up under the mantelpiece, next to our lovely bell chime. There seemed to be a constant mist of sugar and spices in the air, the sweet smell of baking and the lingering taste of icing sugar.

I loved the Christmas biscuits as much for the joy of being able to help make them as for the pleasure of eating them afterwards

Of all the things we had to eat, Omama's Christmas biscuits were by far the best. It is funny how history repeats itself: I can remember my mother phoning Corrado and her cousin Franzi in early December when I was little, checking the ingredients with them, just as I do now with Jem and my mother. I loved the Christmas biscuits as much for the joy of being able to help make them as for the pleasure of eating them afterwards. We started thinking about them at least three weeks before Christmas, but never got round to making them until Jem and I had broken up from school.

My mother would set all the ingredients out on the kitchen table and give us each a wax apron to wear. When I was very little, I was the official decorator, rolling the chocolate biscuits in sugar and topping each one with a glacé cherry or roasted hazelnut. I was allowed to spread the jam on our Spitzbuben and cut the Zimt Sterne into star shapes, threading coloured ribbon through a hole in the top, ready to hang from the tree. The whole biscuit-making process took almost a whole day, with Jem and I rolling the dough for the Vanillepretzel into thin sausages and shaping them into letters and pretzels for what seemed like hours. But it was one of those traditions we all loved to do together, and now that we are all older we still try and meet up at my parents' house early enough to help make them. I remember one year, when I was at university, coming home to find my mother had already made the biscuits without me and feeling terribly cheated.

The chocolate ones are always the first to go and it wasn't uncommon for my mother to make a second batch so there would be enough on Christmas Day. But I love them all and think a few of each on a plate make the perfect accompaniment to a Christmas game of Schwartz Peter.

Of all the things my mother made at Christmas, by far the most elaborate were her gingerbread Hansel and Gretel houses. I have since seen gingerbread house moulds in the shops, but she used to make the whole thing herself, putting her delicate artistry to good use. She started by baking the gingerbread, which always reminded me of the honeyed Lebkuchen slabs Franzi bought us in Switzerland. When it was done, she would cut it into thin squares and set about decorating it, sticking the walls together with caramel and painting little windows, bricks and a door with a paintbrush and some melted cooking chocolate. She piped white icing around the edge and used melted sugar and food colouring to make red and white striped candy canes to hang on the sides. It was one of her most ingenious creations and I can still remember looking at it in the half light from the tree on Christmas morning, mesmerised and lost in a world of fairy tales and make-believe.

I have only made it a handful of times as it is so time-consuming, but a glass of mulled wine seems to make the time go quicker and the end result is never disappointing. If you have the time, and energy, simply make double the quantity of Nonna's Honigleckerli and bake it about 2 cm (inch) thick. Decorate with marzipan, candy canes and chocolate icing and fill with marzipan fruits and chocolate gold coins. Be creative and use sugar-coated pebbles, if you can find them, to make a path leading to the house and dust with icing sugar for a snowy finish.

It was one of her most ingenious creations and I can still remember looking at it in the half light from the tree on Christmas morning, mesmerised and lost in a world of fairy tales and make-believe.

As Christmas day approached, everyone got terribly excited and there was usually a flurry of activity as we busied ourselves wrapping presents and draping tinsel and paper chains from the banisters. I have such fond memories of sitting at the kitchen table in the afternoon after school, a slice of panforte and a mug of cocoa in front of me as I made cards for my family. When I'd finished, I'd put them with the presents in the dining room, ready for Christmas Eve.

We ate a traditional Italian Christmas Eve meal of tortellini in brodo with a glass of watered-down wine, but my parents were always eager to pack us off to bed early so they could make a start on the tree decorating.

Nothing compares to the feeling you get on Christmas morning as a child, the magic and wonder that has the power to bring stories to life and fill any home with festive cheer. For me, the taste of Omama's chocolate biscuits always brings those happy memories flooding back, the smell of vanilla and cinnamon coating everything with a wintry sweetness which I love to this day and always seem to have such a craving for when I'm on a beach somewhere in the height of summer.

We all spent Christmas together in Schonortli one year, when I was nine. I remember feeling nothing could be more special than the sparkling crystals of snow underfoot as we all walked down to the linden trees, our little lanterns lighting the path in front of us. We drank mulled wine and ate fondue by the fire in the living room on Christmas Eve that year and sang carols together by the piano in the *Spielzimmer* before bed. I realised then, looking at the expression of joy on my mother's face, how hard it must have been for her to leave her home. But time makes adventurers of us all, and when I was 17 I begged and pleaded with my parents to let me go away without them for the first time.

CHAPTER 15:

Oysters & Mendiants

*I*t must have been hard for my mother to let me go away on my own. Some of the greatest adventurers the world has known were Italians, but most of the ones I knew preferred to stay near home. There is a heart to an Italian family which seems to beat to a different drum when everyone is close by and although my mother moved away from her home to start a new life in England, her sense of duty and tradition have always remained as strong as the bond she shares with her family.

I think in the end, the only reason she agreed was that she thought it would be good for my French. The language assistant at my school, a university student called Sandrine, had offered for a friend and myself to stay with her and her family in La Rochelle for two weeks and my mother had high hopes I would come back fluent.

La Rochelle is a beautiful port in the Charante-Maritime *département* of western France and Sandrine had made it sound idyllic, telling me about the vineyards and oyster beds, of looking out over the old harbour and drinking citron pressé with her friends in the evenings, and travelling by boat to ile d'Aix where Napoleon spent his last days. I must admit the allure of nights without curfews and days sunning myself on the beach was probably a stronger incentive to me then than the chance to learn about the city's military history. But whatever I said to my mother, it worked, and before I knew it, I was on the plane – dreaming of eating *soupe de poissons* and buttered baguettes as the sun set over the Atlantic.

Sandrine lived most of the year with her mother and stepfather in their farmhouse just outside the town and we were due to spend the first week there and the second with her father at his home near the old harbour in the city's historic centre. As she drove us to her mother's house, she pointed out some of the sights – showing us the 14th-century stone towers which guard the old port, and telling us that Sartre had gone to school there, and that Voltaire and Rabelais had once walked through the old arcaded streets of the city centre. I sat back and let my head fill with romantic notions of sipping *chocolat chaud* in the mornings and chattering away in perfect French.

The farmhouse where Sandrine had grown up was breathtaking. It smelt old with the charming scent of cold stone and moss which permeated the fresh country air. The rooms were basic and the bathroom had little more than an old clawed bath, a basic sink and a toilet. But when I woke up on my first morning there, I understood why she loved it so much. Flinging the wooden shutters open to see a glorious hazy sun and fields of fruit trees and poppies, I felt I was back in Schonortli.

Breakfast was early, as the sun was rising, and there was still an icy bite to the air. Sandrine's mother was a small woman with flame-red, frizzy hair and sharp blue eyes. She offered us fresh baguettes with home-made plum jam which we dunked into bowls of *chocolat chaud*. She drank coffee instead, black and strong, but I preferred the chocolate drink, which she made with dark chocolate shavings melted in a pan of fresh thick milk.

We spent most of the morning at one of the beaches on the ile de Ré and by the time we got home, it was almost siesta time. Sandrine's grandfather was visiting and we were invited to share a drink with them in the garden. I was handed a glass of something cloudy and odd-smelling – it tasted like the liquorice bark my mother sometimes gave Jem and I to suck on when we were little and I gulped it down, not realising it was alcoholic. Before long, the combination of the strong Pernod and the hot afternoon sun had gone to my head and I felt my legs about to give way. Fortunately Sandrine's mother had made a delicious almond tart to soak up some of my headiness and I sat in the shade, one of Sandrine's old sun hats on my head, and let *'l'heure de pastis'* wash over me.

Almond tarts are as common in some parts of France as tea and toast in England, and the French often buy the *pâté brisée* pastry base from the *boulangerie*, just like my mother and Aunt Satu did for their Kuchen in Schonortli. *Pâté brisée* is the French version of shortcrust pastry, but somehow manages to be more buttery and a little lighter than the versions of it you can buy in England. Sandrine's mother made hers with some grated bitter chocolate to give it a richer, fuller flavour which complements the almonds perfectly. What we didn't manage to eat then, she heated on the stove for dinner and served warm with fresh cream and cinnamon sugar.

She refused to give me her recipe, claiming it was a hand-me-down from her great grandmother, but I got a similar one from a stallholder at a Christmas market in Nanterre Ville years later, and have used it ever since on warm summer evenings.

Chocolate & Almond Tart

1 quantity of my mother's sweet shortcrust pastry
   (page 142)

For the frangipane
175 g (6 oz) caster sugar
175 g (6 oz) unsalted butter, softened
3 eggs, beaten
1 tablespoon plain flour
2 tablespoons rum
175 g (6 oz) ground almonds

For the filling
200 ml (7 fl oz) double cream
300 g (10½ oz) dark chocolate
3 egg yolks
30 g (1¼ oz) unsalted butter
150 g (5½ oz) caramelised
   almonds (page 31), crushed

*Preheat the oven to Gas Mark 4/
180°C/fan oven 160°C.*

*To make the frangipane, whisk the sugar and
butter until light and fluffy. Add the eggs and flour
slowly, then the rum, and finally fold in the almonds.*

*Roll out the pastry to fit a 28-cm (11-inch) flan tin.
Bake blind for 15 minutes, then leave to cool.*

*Spread the frangipane over the bottom of the tart case
when cool.*

*Heat the cream and pour over the chocolate. Add the
egg yolks and butter while still hot, then fold in the nuts
and stir well. Pour over the frangipane and leave to cool.*

Set in the fridge for at least an hour before serving.

Serves 8

Staying with Sandrine and her family gave me a taste for French living and I felt a sense of calm and tranquillity I wasn't used to in London. Here life seemed to roll to a slower rhythm and people took time over their food and wine, savouring the taste and enjoying the simplicity good ingredients afford. Her mother was a basic cook, but her dishes were always oozing with taste and local charm. She made crêpes for dinner some nights and topped them with one of her own flavoured sugars which she kept in jars on the window ledge in her kitchen. Some had cinnamon sticks and star anise inside, others vanilla pods, and one had crushed black cardamom seeds which she used to make a chocolate and cardamom Torte on our last day there.

On warm nights, we all ate outside with tea-light candles lighting the path around the garden table and little glass lamps hanging from the branches of the pear and apple trees. The fruit she didn't use fresh on the day, she turned into jams or pickles, and when we left she gave me a jar of preserved lemons made with fresh sea salt and garlic. I watched as she showed me how to caramelise oranges and peaches, cutting thin juliennes of the rind and boiling them in sugar and water, then leaving them to soak overnight – just as my mother had done for her chocolate-coated orange peel. It was an idyllic lifestyle and one I envied terribly, hoping I would one day have the time to make my own cooking ingredients as she had.

People took time over their food and wine, savouring the taste and enjoying the simplicity good ingredients afford

At Sandrine's house, most of the dishes we ate were savoury – basic French meals that were cooked quickly and eaten slowly. But her mother did make a few concessions to my sweet tooth, one of which was a Tarte Tatin made with caramelised apples and pears which was heart-warmingly good – especially served hot with thick fresh cream. She made it seem like the simplest thing on earth to prepare and we chatted in the kitchen as she tossed the chunks of fruit in some vanilla sugar and rolled out a circle of *pâté brisée* to go on top. As we ate it, I realised why the dish has long been one of the mainstays of all good French menus. Legend has it, that it was invented by two sisters at their restaurant in Lamotte-Beuvron. The owner of Paris's famous eatery

Maxim's soon heard of the delicious Tarte Tatin everyone was talking about and sent his spies down to sample it. They came back with the recipe and it has been on the menu at Maxim's ever since. There's no point trying to convince yourself that the fruit makes it healthy, but it makes the perfect ending to a rustic evening meal.

Before setting off from home, my mother had given me two pieces of advice: eat as much seafood as you can and don't drink too much wine. When I told Sandrine, she said she had already planned a day trip for us which would accommodate one, but not the other, of my mother's wishes – La Rochelle's annual oysters and wine festival. Each year, big wooden benches with basic white tablecloths are laid out in the town's historic centre and visitors come and help themselves to as many oysters, mussels and slices of French bread as they can eat. By the time we arrived, just before midday, most of the seats were taken and we had to squeeze in next to a group of American tourists. *Des huîtres* (oysters) are an acquired taste, something for a palate a little more sophisticated than mine was then, and I found myself leaving most of them on the side of my dish. But the mussels were delicious – fresh and garlicky – and we washed the meal down with table glasses of young white wine from the surrounding vineyards. Before long I felt my head start to spin in a way which was becoming all too familiar on this trip.

We moved, once the seafood course was over, to a smaller table with a little metal dish at one end. On top of the dish was a small cluster of dark round discs. These, I later learnt, were mendiants – thin tablets of tempered chocolate with a variety of different toppings. They're eaten at Christmas in Provence where each different decoration is said to represent the four mendicant monastic orders. These ones were made with caramelised hazelnuts and almonds, thin slices of orange peel and pistachio nuts. They're the perfect antidote to the saltiness of the oysters and a great way to make simple chocolate look special. I make them with all sorts of flavourings and sometimes just speckle some gold leaf on top for a Christmas gift. It's so much fun to experiment with them and these, although a little extravagant, are my favourites. Eat them with a glass of Pineau des Charentes – a fortified wine made with local cognac and Sauterne grapes.

SAFFRON-INFUSED MENDIANTS WITH CRUSHED PEPPER & EDIBLE GOLD LEAF

a few strands of Spanish saffron
200 g (7 oz) good-quality dark chocolate
some freshly milled black pepper
edible gold leaf, to decorate

Toast the saffron strands lightly under a grill and pound into a powder in a mortar and pestle.

Melt the chocolate in a bain-marie and add the saffron and a few twists of pepper. Cool and then return to the heat, to temper.

Drop teaspoons of the chocolate on to a sheet of greaseproof paper and sprinkle with gold leaf.

Allow to set before eating.

By the time our first week was up, we had eaten enough good food to last us the rest of our trip, which was a good thing as Sandrine's father was slightly less adept in the kitchen than her mother! He made us a good hare stew on our first night there, with a lot of help from Sandrine, but after that we ate most of our meals in restaurants and cafés. One lunchtime he took us to a little brasserie in Île de Ré for *soupe de poissons* – a delicious fish soup with local prawns, mussels and oysters and a spoonful of pistou (French pesto) to give it extra body and flavour. We ate slices of pissaladière, a simple pizza from the South of France made with anchovies, olives and fresh herbs, which we bought from a street vendor by the harbour after a day at the beach, and drank pastis – which I was slowly developing a taste for – as the sun was setting.

There is a headiness to holiday memories which is just like the feeling you get when you fall in love for the first time or drink a glass of wine on an empty stomach. I grew up a bit on that trip and realised for the first time that there was a whole world out there and that I wanted to see it. When I thought of my mother, it was no longer with a sense of childlike dependence, but more an easy respect – like two women becoming friends for the first time. But it wasn't until I set off for my year abroad, two years later, that I discovered just how strong our bond was.

CHAPTER 16:

Galettes & Grenobloise

*If you are lucky enough to have
lived in Paris as a young man,
then wherever you go for the
rest of your life, it stays with
you, for Paris is a moveable feast.*

ERNEST HEMINGWAY

I remember a little wooden doll – about the size of my thumb – with a blue and white gingham dress and red apron. I must have been eight or nine, too old for dolls really, but this one was special because it had come all the way from Paris. My father often went there on business trips when we were young, meeting with cloth agents and attending that season's fashion shows. He always came back with stories of window-shopping and people-watching, his two favourite pastimes, and a bottle of my mother's favourite perfume. But this time she went with him, and when they got back she brought it to life for Jem and me the same way she always did, by telling us stories. We listened as she told us about eating roasted chestnuts and watching the sunset from the top of the Eiffel Tower. Impatient to hear more, I laughed as she and my father argued about whether the sky had been a Burnt Sienna or Indian Yellow that day, and I remember how she leant in close as she described the artists in Place de Théâtre and the smell of honeyed almonds wafting through the cool carnival air. There was an aura of romance to her memories, like someone talking about a loved one far away, and I longed to go and see it for myself.

My chance finally came when I was 17 and my parents invited me to join them on one of my father's business trips. It was late April and I was halfway through my first year of sixth form. I had papers to write and exams to prepare for, but I jumped at the chance to take two days off school and go with them. My father had work during the day, leaving my mother and me free to sightsee, sip *chocolat ancien* and eat galettes as we strolled over the Pont Neuf together. Everything was just as she had described it, a city in love with love, oozing style from every pore – even the Metro stations were a work of art with their little art deco details and ornate street signs.

We were staying in a small auberge near Place de la Concorde, with high ceilings and polished floorboards. My room overlooked a courtyard and in the mornings I could hear the chef shouting to the waiters to 'pick-up', as the smell of fresh *pain au chocolat* wafted pleasantly through the air.

We must have walked miles in those few days: up the steps to the Sacré Coeur, down again to Montmartre where we found a cavernous art gallery showing a Chagall exhibition. We went to the very top of the Eiffel Tower and felt it sway in the wind, and in the evening, before meeting my father, we strolled through St-Germain and drank citron pressé and ate a dish of the most delicious vanilla biscuits I have ever tasted. They were so rich I could smell the butter and they were drizzled with dark and white chocolate. I searched high and low for this recipe and it was eventually given to me by a French pastry chef at a restaurant where I waitressed in Sydney. The biscuits always come out beautifully, as long as the butter is ice cold, but if the mixture doesn't resemble breadcrumbs somehow the whole thing refuses to work.

Chocolate-coated Vanilla Biscuits

350 g (12 oz) '00' plain cake flour
a pinch of salt
a pinch of cinnamon
200 g (7 oz) ice-cold unsalted butter, grated
200 g (7 oz) vanilla sugar (page 242)
1 egg, beaten
100 g (3½ oz) white cooking chocolate
100 g (3½ oz) dark cooking chocolate

Sift the flour, salt and cinnamon and add the butter and sugar, mixing with your fingertips until it resembles fine breadcrumbs.

Add the egg and mix well into a firm dough. Wrap in clingfilm and chill for 30 minutes.

Preheat the oven to Gas Mark 3/160°C/fan oven 140°C.

Roll out on a floured surface and cut with biscuit cutters into 2.5-cm (1-inch) circles about 5 mm (¼ inch) thick.

Bake on a buttered tray for 20 minutes and leave to cool.

When they have cooled, melt the dark and white chocolate in separate bowls. Dip some of the biscuits into the white chocolate to coat, then drizzle with the dark chocolate for a striped effect. Dip the remaining biscuits in the dark chocolate and drizzle with the white. Leave to set.

Makes about 50

In the evenings we all went to dinner with Serge, an old friend and work colleague of my father's, who took great delight in showing us his city's best haunts. I ate pâté de fois gras for the first time, spread on hot toast, and crêpes with Grand Marnier and sugar, flambéd at our table. As I sat in my room on our last night, listening to the sound of traffic in the distance and the bustle from the street below, I vowed to come back one day. I wanted to feel at home there, to be one of those chic young ladies dashing home from work on the Metro and to wake up each morning to the smell of roasting coffee and freshly baked bread. If I'd known then what the future would bring, I would have sat back and relaxed, enjoying my last night, but instead I looked at the starry Parisian sky with a sadness I hadn't felt before, a longing almost for somewhere I thought should be home...

When I arrived at Nanterre, suddenly unsure of my shaky language skills, I realised that this was not the place I had been dreaming about for the last three years

I arrived in Paris for the second time, early in the morning, cold, tired and hungry. I'd been on a coach for the best part of 11 hours and had eaten my way through my mother's packed lunch in the first 20 minutes. I was an impoverished language student at Reading university and this was the first day of my year abroad – a far cry from the idyllic holiday trip I'd taken with my parents almost three years earlier. I remember feeling pure joy when I learnt there was a place for me at the Paris X University in Nanterre and my hands were shaking when I circled the courses I wanted to take while I was there: romantic literature of the 19th century, Italian-French translation, and philosophy. I dreamt then, not for the first time, of being a writer, holed up in a little garret somewhere on the Left Bank, scribbling down ideas for novels on the back of an old copy of *Paris Match* and drinking red wine from a wide glass.

But when I arrived at Nanterre, suddenly unsure of my shaky language skills, I realised that this was not the place I had been dreaming about for the last three years. The campus was a grey mass of concrete tower blocks and graffitied wire bike sheds and my digs were no better. There was a group of four or five of us from the same university and we were all allocated rooms in a hall of residence with only one kitchen and bathroom to share between 30 or so students. I sat on my bed, my packed suitcase at my feet, and felt a pang of homesickness so strong I could feel the tears welling up. I thought of my mother, alone in London at 25, and Nonna in Milan and wondered why we had all wanted to go so far from what we knew and loved.

But in the end, all it took was a knock at my door to lift my spirits. A Spanish girl called Belene said she had seen me arrive and wanted to invite me to have dinner with her and her friends in the kitchen. Between her pigeon French and my faltering Italian we managed to make ourselves understood and I grabbed a bottle of cheap wine I'd bought at the coach station and followed her down the corridor. When I got there, the tiny room was already full of students, French, Italian, Spanish, German, all chattering in a friendly hybrid of all four languages. I instantly felt at home when I saw a large pan of rich tomatoey sugo bubbling away on the hob and before long, a dreadlocked Italian boy called Marco was playing the guitar and everyone was having a good time. It was the first time, outside the familiar environment of my own home, that I realised what an important mediator food could be.

It was the first time, outside the familiar environment of my own home, that I realised what an important mediator food could be

I have many happy memories of that kitchen, from eating Buccatini alla Taormina on someone's birthday to having chocolate fondue on New Year's Eve, drinking good table wine and singing 'Hotel California' at the top of our voices. At first I felt a little self-conscious about cooking in the presence of so many Mediterraneans. But I had my chance to prove myself on Belene's birthday. I spent hours in that kitchen, melting bitter chocolate, grinding almonds and whisking eggs to make my Nonna's Napoleon's Torte, which I loved to eat warm from the oven with a dollop of fresh cream. For the icing I carefully tempered the fine Lindt chocolate I'd bought that day, adding a spoonful of butter as my mother always did and watching as the gloss spread across the top of the bowl. I poured it slowly over a thin layer of apricot jam and smoothed it down with the back of my spoon. The cake was a huge success, though as I ate it, I couldn't avoid the familiar pangs of homesickness and longed to be sharing it with my own family.

NONNA'S NAPOLEON'S TORTE

4 large eggs, separated
150 g (5^1/$_2$ oz) caster sugar
150 g (5^1/$_2$ oz) unsalted butter
2 tablespoons self-raising flour
50 g (1^3/$_4$ oz) breadcrumbs
150 g (5^1/$_2$ oz) ground almonds
80 g (3 oz) dark cooking chocolate
      (we only ever use Lindt Excellence for this recipe)
apricot jam
For Omama's Chocoladeglasur (chocolate glaze)
80 g (3 oz) dark chocolate
30 g (1^1/$_4$ oz) butter
60 g (2 oz) icing sugar, sifted

Preheat the oven to Gas Mark 5/190°C/fan oven 170°C.

Cream the egg yolks and sugar until light and fluffy. Sift the flour and mix in slowly with the breadcrumbs and almonds.

Melt the chocolate in a bain-marie. Whisk the egg whites until stiff. Fold alternate spoonfuls of each mixture into the creamed mixture until there is none left.

Put into a greased and lined 20-cm (8-inch) cake tin and bake for 40 minutes, checking after 30 minutes. Leave to cool on a rack.

When cool, spread the top of the cake with a thin layer of apricot jam.

To make the glaze, melt the chocolate in a bain-marie with 2 tablespoons of water, the butter and icing sugar. Pour over the top and leave to set.

As I grew more comfortable in my surroundings, I decided to explore, starting with Nanterre Ville – a picturesque, cobbled village one stop further out of the city on the Metro. It was late November and bitterly cold, but when I arrived my spirits instantly rose. It looked like a happy Christmas scene from one of my favourite Advent calendars: tiny, slightly lop-sided shops with lead-framed windows and decorations hanging up inside. There was a warm orange glow from street lamps and lanterns and the welcoming smell of freshly baked *pain d'épices* cut through the icy air. I had only a few francs on me, so I bought a paper cornet of roasted chestnuts and a cup of *chocolat chaud* before heading off.

From then on, trips to Nanterre Ville became a regular Sunday morning treat. I usually met up with friends and our first stop would be the morning markets for our weekly food shopping. I filled my string bag with succulent asparagus, beef tomatoes, frisée salad, and haricot beans so ripe and fat they looked like my favourite marzipan shapes from the sweet shops in Switzerland.

It was only a small village but the locals were always busy, rushing from shop to shop getting everything they needed for Sunday lunch and it was hard not to get caught up in the hurried flow. We went to the *charcuterie* for bacon and meat for lunch, then to the *fromagerie* for ripe country Brie and juniper berry jelly and a fat sausage of goat's cheese which I loved to eat warm with salad and toast. But the best, as usual, had been saved for last – the patisserie. I never bought the same thing twice, promising myself I would try everything while I had the chance, but my favourite was the Tarte Grenobloise. I had had it only once before, on my holiday in La Rochelle, but here it was made with the creamiest nutty chocolate ganache. Monday mornings for me meant an 8 a.m. start with two hours of French to Italian translation, so I knew I would need something special on Sunday night to give me sweet dreams. This was just the thing. I waited in line as the customers in front of me shouted out their orders: '*Tarte aux pommes*', '*Tarte aux fraises*', '*Eclairs*', '*Gâteau*'.

> Monday mornings for me meant an 8 a.m. start with two hours of French to Italian translation, so I knew I would need something special on Sunday night to give me sweet dreams

It all looked mouthwateringly good and when it came to my turn I had a hard job exercising any amount of self-restraint. '*Deux tranches de Tarte Grenobloise,*' I shouted confidently and the lady sliced the gooey cake with a heavy carving knife and wrapped each piece in wax paper. The caramelised pecans on top glowed like gold in the cold blue air and I could almost taste the chocolate filling.

Tarte Grenobloise is the easiest dessert to make yourself at home, once you have overcome the urge to eat most of the ganache before it reaches the tart. This is my own simple version, which I like to serve with a strong espresso to balance some of that creamy sweetness. It's also good with a glass of amaretto.

TARTE GRENOBLOISE

1 quantity of my mother's sweet shortcrust pastry
    (page 142)
200 ml (7 fl oz) double cream
250 g (9 oz) dark cooking chocolate
100 g (3½ oz) whole pecans
100 g (3½ oz) whole sweet almonds
about 4 tablespoons caster sugar

Preheat the oven to Gas Mark 4/180°C/fan oven 160°C.

Roll out the pastry to fit a 23-cm (9-inch) flan tin and bake the pastry blind for 15–20 minutes.

To make the ganache, heat the cream in a heavy-bottomed pan and pour over the chocolate, stirring constantly until it has melted. Fill the pastry case with the chocolate ganache and put in the refrigerator to set.

Meanwhile, make the croccante by placing the nuts on a sheet of greaseproof paper. Melt the sugar in a heavy-bottomed pan until dissolved and a clear caramel and quickly pour over the nuts. Leave to set.

When the croccante has set, crush into small pieces and sprinkle over the top of the tart.

Serves 6–8

When we couldn't carry any more shopping, we'd make our way to the galette man for breakfast. He looked like one of those kindly grandfathers you see in French text books at school, rosy cheeked and red nosed, a tuft of milky white hair escaping from under his train-driver's cap. His sleeves were rolled up no matter how cold it was outside and all morning he would be mixing the buckwheat batter and tossing the thick pancakes into the air. The smell was divine – a sweet, cinnamon aroma with a hint of cocoa and butter. I would order mine and watch as he mixed, fried and flipped it over his tiny stove. The result was thick and chocolatey, crispy on the outside and soft and gooey in the middle. He would sprinkle it with icing sugar, top it with a generous knob of butter and hand it to me in a paper cone. You can't help but get sweet butter on your chin as you eat these and even though they are the size of a large dinner plate, they somehow always leave you wanting more.

The campus at Nanterre was always awake early and, as most of my lectures started at 8 a.m., so was I. Dragging myself out of bed at that time for lessons that I was still struggling with was not the highlight of my day, but breakfast at the station soon made up for it. The little bread stall could have easily been overlooked. Standing in one corner of the dreary train station, the first time I saw it I assumed it would be a poor imitation of the wonderful shops I'd already seen dotted around the city. But one morning, a rumbling in my stomach and a bad case of homesickness made me stop there for a hot chocolate and croissant. The menu, scrawled in a child's hand on a dusty blackboard, listed all the usual breakfast choices, but something at the bottom caught my eye: 'Pain Viennoise au Chocolat'.

I ordered one and a *chocolat chaud*, by now my favourite drink at any time of day. I was handed a baguette and small paper cup. I was in a hurry and ate as I walked but when I tasted the bread I had to stop for a moment to appreciate it properly. The baguette was light and sweet, like a brioche but less dense. It simply melted in the mouth and the chocolate chunks were still warm and soft from the oven. The combination of tastes and textures was incredible and yet so simple. I took my time walking to my lecture that morning, and when I arrived I felt I was ready for anything.

Mastering the bread for this breakfast dish can be a little tricky, but the secret is to make sure you mix the fresh yeast with warm milk; cold milk will leave you with a hard stone-like loaf.

Use chunks of dark chocolate if you can, rather than commercial chocolate chips, as they melt better while still retaining some of their shape.

MELTING CHOCOLATE CHIP PAIN VIENNOISE – FOR COLD MORNINGS

2 teaspoons dried yeast
300 ml (10 fl oz) full-cream milk
500 g (1 lb 2 oz) strong white bread flour
1^1/$_2$ teaspoons salt
60 g (2 oz) unsalted butter, creamed
1 teaspoon granulated sugar
2 tablespoons kirsch
150 g (5^1/$_2$ oz) dark chocolate chunks
For the glaze
1 egg yolk
1 tablespoon milk

Sprinkle the yeast into 100 ml (3^1/$_2$ fl oz) of the warm milk and leave for a few minutes.

Sift the flour and salt into a bowl and make a well in the centre. Pour in the yeasted milk and slowly draw enough of the flour in from the edges to form a paste. Cover with a damp tea towel and leave until frothy and risen – about 20 minutes.

Slowly pour half of the remaining milk into the well and mix in the flour, butter, sugar, kirsch and chocolate chunks. Add the rest of the milk as required to form a dough. Knead well until shiny and then put in a clean bowl and cover with a tea towel. Leave until it has doubled in size – about 2 hours.

Preheat the oven to Gas Mark 4/180°C/fan oven 160°C.

Knock back by punching the dough in the middle to deflate it and leave to rest for 10 minutes.

Plait the dough or roll it into a long baguette. Mix the ingredients for the glaze and brush over the shaped dough. Bake for 35–40 minutes.

The weeks leading up to Christmas seemed to fly by and soon it was time to pack my things and catch the coach home. I couldn't have been more excited and had been dreaming about seeing my parents and eating a proper Christmas dinner for ages. My mother met me at the station with a wide embrace and on the way home we chatted excitedly, catching up on each other's news. Soon Nanterre and translation classes seemed like a distant memory.

We all sat down that evening to a slice of panforte and a glass of mulled wine, enjoying the lazy holiday feeling. But I had exams coming up in January and four days later I was back on the coach, heading for Paris once again, my head full of warm memories and my bags full of panettone, Omama's biscuits, mince pies and Christmas cake.

Despite my sadness at leaving home after such a short break, I was looking forward to my first New Year's Eve in Paris. The hall of residence had been decorated with paper lanterns and tinsel and in the kitchen some of the Italians were already busy preparing for the big night. There were posters up in the corridor for the Fondue Fête and everyone was invited, provided we all bring something to the party.

Marco and some of the other Italians usually spent their winters skiing in Italy or Switzerland so had been brought up on fondue parties, and when I woke the next morning there was an insistent knocking at my door.

Em (left) enjoying a fondue with me on New Year's Eve

Apparently my job was to write the forfeits. No proper fondue is complete without penalties for dropping your chunk of bread in the cheese. I remembered the forfeits at a fondue party my family had had in Schonortli one year. I had been nine and I will never forget the embarrassment at my first penalty: having to count backwards from 100 in Italian. I spent the rest of the day coming up with suitable ideas, writing them on small pieces of torn scrap paper and folding them into an old tophat.

That afternoon a few of us went to Nanterre Ville for supplies: fresh baguettes for dipping, cornichons, capers, potatoes, herbs, garlic and salami which would all be chopped into small cubes and served with toothpicks as an hors d'oeuvre. Then there was the fondue: comté, Gruyère and Emmenthal were the favourite choice of cheese, plus kirsch and white wine for cooking and plenty of champagne and wine to wash it down. I already had plans for dessert – a chocolate fondue made with fine dark chocolate and rum.

The evening was one of the most memorable I have ever had, with everyone in high spirits, wine flowing and the sound of laughter as people nudged each other into dropping their pieces of bread in the fondue. By the time we reached dessert we were already full, but the smell of the molten chocolate and liqueur soon revived our appetites and before long it was all gone.

Fondue is the easiest thing in the world to make as long as you have the right ingredients and a good atmosphere. Just remember to serve it with wine as water will react with the cheese or chocolate to form a large uncomfortable ball in your stomach.

CHOCOLATE FONDUE WITH FRUIT & BISCOTTI DIPPERS

400 g (14 oz) dark cooking chocolate
100 ml (3½ fl oz) single cream
4 tablespoons dark rum
1 small packet of chocolate-chip biscotti
4 firm bananas, cut into quarters
about 250 g (9 oz) large strawberries
a few chunks of tinned pineapple
3 firm pears, cored and quartered

Melt the chocolate, cream and rum in a fondue pot or heavy-bottomed saucepan and keep warm over a flame.

Break up the biscotti and arrange with the fruit on a dish. Serve immediately.

Serves 8–10

I was so grateful for my new friends that night, but also for my memories of home: the two were coming together more and more each day, helping me to make sense of things and giving me the confidence to discover who I really was. I realised then, for the first time, that I could do it on my own, but only because I knew there would be people to catch me if I fell, and as I prepared to start the second part of my year abroad – in Rome – I felt more confident and at ease than I had in a long time.

CHAPTER 17:

Mamma Figlia

I remember many things about my nonno: the way he folded his arms in front of him when he was nervous, or how he waved his finger at us when he was angry, and the serenity in his eyes when he smiled at my mother. But one of the things I remember most about him is that he always kept a copy of the Bible and Dante's *Divina Commedia* at his bedside. He had spent his whole life studying them and would quote Dante for almost every occasion. When I told him I was going to live in Rome as part of my year abroad, he reminded me of Dante – lost in a dark wood – and advised me to always remain humble and think of the lessons my parents had taught me.

I suppose a big motivation behind my decision to study Italian was the desire to be even closer to my family. As a girl I was always shy, and being able to understand only a handful of words at the dinner table in Schonortli didn't help. I wanted to be able to take part in the conversation like Silvia, to feel that I really belonged. Learning another language is as liberating as learning how to swim or drive or ride a bike – it gives you a freedom to understand other cultures and feel at home in other countries and I had romantic dreams of phoning my mother from Rome and chattering away in Italian, enjoying a new level of closeness with her.

I had to enrol in two classes at La Sapienza, Rome's main university, and I chose Dante's *Inferno* and the history of art in Rome's churches. Before I set off, Corrado sent me a beautiful antique edition of the *Commedia*, which I packed in my suitcase along with the line drawing my father had done of Fiascherino when I was a girl and a silver locket my mother had given me on my 16th birthday. Armed with my memories and the recipe books I had been adding to over the years, I felt calm and ready for the months ahead.

I was becoming used to leaving one place and starting again in another, but nothing prepares you for the sensation you feel in the pit of your stomach when you realise you're leaving behind the people you love most. I told my mother this the week before I was due to leave and the next day she came into my room and sat on the corner of the bed. 'I'll come with you.' I knew from the defiant look in her eyes that there was nothing I could do to convince her I would be all right and deep down I didn't want to. She booked us into a pensione off Piazza Repubblica, near Termini – Rome's main train station – and suddenly my nerves turned to excitement and we giggled like schoolgirls as we stepped off the plane into the familiar heat of Italy.

We had arrived early in the evening, the day before my 21st birthday, and the air had a warmth to it which was both stifling and, strangely, a comfort. It smelt Roman – that intangible scent only ancient cities seem to have, a little like roasting coffee beans and salty sea water. We checked in and headed straight out again, keen to make the most of our first evening while the city was still bathed in a delicious salmon-pink glow. There is an edginess to Termini and the surrounding *vincoli*, a confusing allure which can be both welcoming and hostile. For me, it conjures up the very essence of Rome: a paradox of a city which manages to be both the country's religious epicentre and also host to the world's greatest monuments to barbarism and violence. The Colosseum stands at its centre, a simple crucifix casting a shadow over the arena where so many Christians lost their lives, and the churches at every turn boast artworks which are reminders of both the city's greatness and the papacy's corruption.

We walked under the bridge to the Vittorio Emmanuele building – 'the wedding cake' as my Italian friends called it; a frilly confection of a building which gleams pure white in the midday sun but seemed almost tired when we saw it that first evening. I felt intimidated and awed by the baroque beauty around me and longed for something familiar, so my mother did what we always do when we are in need of some quick comforting – she bought me some chocolate.

We stopped in a little restaurant near Bernini's Four Seasons fountain in Piazza Navona and my mother ordered us a coffee and bar-snack each. The waiter came back with a lukewarm *cappuccino bianca* and little ricotta cheese crostini with dark chocolate shavings sprinkled on top. It was enough – a small kick to get us going. We had found a friend in this imposing city and we began, slowly, to relax.

These crostini are very easy to make and look deceptively sophisticated. I sometimes serve them if I'm having a drinks party and make a few little ricotta pastries on the side.

The Colosseum

CROSTINI WITH CHOCOLATE SHAVINGS –
EAT WHEN SAD

1 small baguette
100 g (3¹/₂ oz) fresh soft ricotta cheese
50 g (1¹/₂ oz) dark chocolate

Simply slice the bread diagonally and thinly. Toast lightly under a medium grill and top with a spoonful of the cheese. Shave slivers of the chocolate on top with a vegetable peeler. Serve warm.

The bars and cafés in Italy often sell *copertura*, chunks of Italian couverture, in jars on the counter, and as we left we bought one each. I had never seen chocolate like that before, in such huge, outsized chunks. The chunks come in white, milk and dark chocolate and, because of the higher fat content, they're unnervingly rich. Most Italians grate and melt them to eat with figs and baked peaches or use them to coat candied fruit and nuts at Christmastime. But that evening we ate them in one go as we walked, feeling thoroughly sick but hugely satisfied at the end of it.

It was late and dark by the time we were returning to the pensione. We were heading down a narrow, dark little *vincolo* when we heard a man's voice calling to us. '*Mamma, figlia?*' (Mother and daughter?) he said as we approached. He must have been at least 80 and was hunched over a broom, hovering by the doorway leading to a little courtyard. As we got closer, we could see that there was a sign outside the gate: '*Aperta*' (open). The man ushered us inside. The room was large and well lit with about eight or nine tables, roughly set with white placemats and table glasses. It must have been the smallest, most basic restaurant I have ever seen and there was only one other customer: a man sitting on his own, eating a plate of veal schnitzel and greens. There were only two dishes and no menu – fish or schnitzel. Dessert was Torta della Nonna and a delicious almond ice cream which the chef's wife had made fresh that day. The cake was moist and rich and I realised then why it has always been one of my father's favourite Italian desserts. There are lots of variations, depending on what's in season, but this one had pine nuts and bitter almonds and a subtle dusting of grated lemon zest on top. We walked back afterwards, full and content, enjoying our new label of 'mamma figlia' and looking forward to spending my birthday together in this magical city.

The next morning, serenaded by the sound of motorinos and car horns, I realised that it would be my first birthday in 21 years without chocolate cake or a home-cooked birthday meal. But my mother promised to make up for it and we agreed to spend the day in Trastevere on the other side of the river. Peppered with little rep cinemas, theatres and restaurants, the studenty district has a casual, artistic feel which reminded me of the Left Bank in Paris and we decided to do some 'people-watching' in the morning and spend the afternoon exploring. Sitting in the main piazza, sipping a *granita di caffè*, we convinced ourselves that no matter how far we travelled, we would always feel close in spirit.

I realised that it would be my first birthday in 21 years without chocolate cake or a home-cooked birthday meal

My mother told me about the first time she left home, to come to London, and how she felt when she realised she wanted to marry my father and stay for good. It was heart wrenching for her, knowing she would never live close to Nonna and Nonno again, but it was also liberating – her first real step into adulthood – and the best part was knowing that everyone was still going to be exactly where she had left them. I thought of that as I watched the people go by and tried to picture my father reading his paper with a slice of toast and honey in the morning, or Jem playing badminton with me in the garden on balmy summer evenings. It was a comfort, she was right, and I felt serene and excited by what the future would bring.

We hunted around for a good place for lunch and in the end settled on a small trattoria set in the remains of an 18th-century palazzo. The walls were frescoed and there were flagstones on the floor, giving the whole place an ancient cavernous feel. We ate Penne Arrabbiata with fried zucchini flowers and for dessert my mother ordered an extravagant chocolate tart. It had a soft bitter pastry case and inside it tasted like pure Nutella.

We spent the rest of the afternoon walking, discovering the best place for traditional Neapolitan pizza, served on thin *'carta della musica'* dough and topped with fresh olives, anchovies and capers, and we found a small, out of the way bar which served delicious *granita di cioccolato* with fresh cream. These little drinks are hard to describe without making them sound too much like slush puppies. They are the simplest thing in the world to make, using just crushed ice and puréed fruit, melted chocolate or coffee and liqueur. I ate mine with a spoon, like an ice cream, enjoying the sensation of feeling at home in a foreign city. I make granitas all year round and have often offered them as accompaniments to desserts instead of cream. Lemon granitas go particularly well with chocolate, but my favourite combination is chocolate granita with a thick slice of fresh Torta della Nonna.

GRANITA DI CIOCCOLATO

700 ml (1½ pints) cocoa, made with full-cream milk,
    cocoa powder and sugar to taste
50 g (1½ oz) dark chocolate, melted and cooled slightly

Let the hot chocolate cool, then place it in an ice tray in the freezer. Scrape it with a fork every now and then to break it up until it forms small crystals.

Pour the melted chocolate on top and serve with fresh whipped cream.

Serves 8

Despite being mid February, the air was warm and dry. I remember feeling happier than I had done in months but also a little lost and vulnerable. I kept thinking of the following day when my mother was due to leave and I would be alone again and I wanted more than anything to hold on to her and beg her to stay. Rome is a great reflector of moods and I found while I was there that it could be happy or sad, depending on how I was feeling. When I felt good, Rome seemed almost to shine with a sunny Mediterranean warmth and when I missed home the stone flagstones felt colder underfoot and the statues and monuments seemed to look down on me with sad eyes.

That afternoon we both felt the sadness in the air and that was when my mother took me to see Santa Cecilia in Trastevere – the most moving of all the statues I saw while I was in Rome. The young saint lies lifeless at the altar, captured in marble by the Italian artist Stefano Maderno. Legend has it that she was martyred for her faith in around AD 230 by three blows to her neck. When Maderno was commissioned to do the sculpture in the late 16th century, he requested to see her body. The casket was opened and there she lay, serene and perfectly preserved, a gold cloth covering her wound. It still makes me cry to think of her today, as I did that afternoon, her head turned modestly away and her arms lying limp by her side.

There was only one cure for us then – food. We decided then and there to have the best meal we could find, something to celebrate my birthday and our time together, something to give us a lasting memory of our Roman holiday. We picked a small restaurant not too far from where we had eaten the night before. It was tucked away in a dark side street, just off the main thoroughfare on Piazza Repubblica and far enough away from the commercial tourist-traps offering 'St Peter's Pizza' and 'Calzone Colosseo'. I don't remember its name but can picture the inside as clearly as if I were looking at a photograph. It was luscious red, like a ripe pomegranate – a surprise after the cracked stone frontage and the mimosa and forget-me-nots tumbling out of pretty little hanging baskets by the entrance.

The heavy wooden door must have been effective soundproofing, because the moment we stepped inside we were hit by a collective noise of cutlery clinking, loud artisan music and excited chatter. The walls were lined with framed pictures of movie stars and celebrities: I half expected to see one of the Pope shaking hands with the owner, or Robert De Niro eating spaghetti and meatballs with a napkin tucked into his shirt. There was an intimacy to it, but also a 1920s-style decadence, and the clientele were as colourful as the decor. We were quickly seated in the centre of the room by a waiter wearing a tuxedo and bow tie. To our left was a small portly man with thinning hair and a three-piece suit, sharing a glass of wine with an Amazonian blonde, who was oozing cleavage and dripping with diamonds. And to our right was a group of dandy young men in velvet jackets and intellectual-looking women wearing kaftans and Indian jewellery.

Our waiter explained that there were no menus and that the restaurant specialised in regional dishes. He told us that he would bring a selection of small plates, rather than the more conventional bowls of pasta and meat you would get in the north. Our first course was creamed spinach and fried zucchini flowers stuffed with ricotta and sepia risotto; next came ravioli stuffed with wild mushrooms and meat, then several platters of chargrilled seafood. Rome isn't renowned for its desserts, but when I saw what we were having, my heart fluttered excitedly. There was a selection of miniature chocolate puddings and cakes, each one bite-sized and beautifully presented. We had little chocolate macaroon balls filled with dark chocolate cream; miniature tarts filled with chocolate and hazelnut paste; a tiny chocolate mille-feuille; and little *iperole* – pastry tubes, lined with dark chocolate and filled with fresh cream. By the end, we were both so full that we needed a glass of grappa to help us breathe again.

It was the best meal I had ever had – better than the ones my parents had treated me to in Paris, better than the tea and cakes at Schuh with Nonna and Nonno, and better even than the delicious meals I had in La Rochelle. It made such an impression on my taste buds that I took my husband there years later, the evening after he proposed to me on bended knee in the Borghesi gardens, as the sun was setting behind the poplar trees. We ate meat skewers and Gnocchi alla Romana and had grilled cheese with honey for dessert; and laughed together at the memory of my mother and me staggering home, so full we could barely walk.

CHAPTER 18:

Food for Friends

Il Caffè Greco è l'unico posto al mondo dove sedersi e aspettar la fine. (The Caffè Greco is the only place in the world where you can sit down and await the end.)

GIORGIO DE CHIRICO

I think that chocolate must share certain attributes with alcohol, because the morning after our big meal my mother and I were both feeling decidedly the worse for wear. The joy we had felt the night before on finding such a good restaurant had been replaced with pounding heads and pale faces. We ate our breakfast and drank our coffee in silence, neither of us wanting to think about the day ahead. But one thing my year abroad was teaching me was how to cope with goodbyes, and as I waved my mother off at the airport later that day I promised myself that I would get the most out of my time there.

And I was fortunate that I was not alone. Corrado had insisted I call if I needed anything and Franzi had put me in touch with a good friend of hers, Fiamma, who lived on the outskirts of Rome. We met up a few weeks later and she showed me some of the best Caravaggios in the world, hidden modestly in a number of the city's more obscure churches. We must have walked for miles that day, and as evening approached we rewarded ourselves with a well-earned drink. Fiamma took me to one of Rome's most infamous literary haunts: the Caffè Greco, where it is said Stendhal and Baudelaire used to go to write and where Hans Christian Andersen lived in one of the rooms upstairs for a time. The walls are decorated with 19th-century landscapes, and there is a saying that if a cardinal walks in there, he will be next in line to become Pope, because that's what happened to Cardinal Gioacchino Pecci who later became Pope Leo XIII.

We drank a thick Florentine hot chocolate with whipped cream. Even though I had already started to make friends and feel a little more at home, the sweet chocolate was a comfort, a reminder of family, and I sipped it slowly. It was a small drink, but so satisfying it left you feeling you had eaten a huge dessert. I like to call my version Espresso di Cioccolata because the ones we had that day were served in small espresso cups and left us with the same excited palpitations. This is another non-recipe, but it's worth mentioning because just one of these will be enough to lift dulled spirits and make foreign places seem familiar.

ESPRESSO DI CIOCCOLATA 'AL GRECO'

60 g (2 oz) dark chocolate
a pinch of cinnamon
50 ml (2 fl oz) full-cream milk

Finely grate the chocolate and add the cinnamon. Put a little of it into an espresso cup – just enough to line the bottom. Heat the milk through and pour over the top, stirring until all the chocolate has melted. Drink hot.

Makes about 8 cups

Making friends in Italy is not so much a skill as a way of life. Everyone you meet, from the person who serves you your morning cappuccino, to the cashier at the supermarket, will have something to add to your day. Sometimes it's just a simple '*Buongiorno*' said when the sun is up and the smell of fresh coffee is in the air, or '*Buon appetito*' as you're about to tuck into your lunchtime bowl of pasta. I had only been in Rome a few weeks and yet already I had met people at the university I knew would become lasting friends, and had more tour-guides and dinner-invites than I knew what to do with.

One of the Italian students I had met in my hall of residence in Paris – Ilaria Navone, a friendly girl with dark hair and a warm smile which made me think of my mother – had moved back to Rome soon after I did and we arranged to meet up. It was fun reminiscing about our fondue party in Nanterre and the time we had all made pasta in the tiny kitchen and she promised to show me some of Rome's best eateries.

The first place she took me to was a little bakery near Piazza Navona. She explained the story behind the famous Bernini fountain while we ate a delicious winter speciality made with fresh ricotta and Nutella. Legend has it that the city's two most talented artists, Bernini and Borromini, hated each other with a passion. Borromini designed the Sant' Agnese church in the centre of the piazza and facing it is Bernini's Four Rivers fountain. The story goes that the figures in the fountain are shielding their eyes in disgust at Borromini's architecture, but the truth is that Bernini finished work on the fountain two years before the church was

'*Scusa, posso comprare un pezzo di pane?*'

built. The figures are actually covering their eyes to indicate that the source of one of the rivers was still undiscovered.

After we had eaten, Ilaria took me to Campo dei Fiori for a sunset drink. The old flower market is surrounded by wine bars serving delicious fresh wines and good bar food. There are still daily fruit and vegetable markets in the square, and if you ask the stallholders nicely, they sometimes give great tips on what to do with the fresh produce. I got my recipes for spinach gnocchi and grilled fennel parmigiana from a cheery, stout little woman there, who, if she wasn't already, looked as if she ought to be someone's nonna. When I told her I had an incurable sweet tooth, she gave me her mother's recipe for chocolate-dipped asparagus. I have never actually made it, but she assured me that the combination of the creamy vegetable and a good dark chocolate was unrivalled.

It was late by the time I said goodbye to Ilaria and as I headed home I felt the familiar rumblings in my stomach which come from too much wine and a childhood of midnight feasts. I had only a few tins of ravioli and some stale bread in my cupboard and decided it was time to see if the *fornaio* - the little bakery below my apartment - kept the same hours as the one near my student house in Reading. I have the best memories of staggering home late from the pub with my housemates – a little the worse for wear and in need of some pre-hangover stodge – and finding that the bakery down the road was just getting a batch of fresh cheese bread out of the oven. They always sold us a couple, hot and melting, which we ate standing up by the fridge, spreading thick knifefuls of butter on to each tiny little morsel. It became a Saturday night ritual and when we left for our various years abroad, we vowed to keep the memory of that year alive by finding a similar night-time 'bread shop'.

I could smell that comforting, homey aroma of baking as I approached. I poked my head tentatively round the corner and saw the baker hard at work, a white apron on and his jet-black hair tied back with an elastic band. '*Scusa, posso comprare un pezzo di pane?*' (Excuse me, can I buy some bread?) I asked. He looked a little surprised at first, but was soon happy for the company and offered me a square of pizza bianca – fresh focaccia with sea salt and rosemary – and a box of *cornetti*, small Italian-style croissants, which he told me to save for breakfast. I knew the Italians often ate these with their morning coffee, and I had had one or two since I arrived, but I had yet to be converted. I decided that if his focaccia was anything to go by, the *cornetti* would be worth trying and gave him a few coins in exchange for six – enough for me and my two new flatmates.

The next morning, as the sun rose over the Tiber and I felt a day closer to being at home in Rome, I got my box of *cornetti* and warmed them in the oven. We ate them with mugs of black coffee and decided then and there that we would never eat anything else. They were filled with a chocolate crème pâtissière, thick and sweet, and the pastry was feather light. They were different from croissants, smaller and sweeter, and we ate the lot before the coffee had cooled. I don't have a recipe for these, simply because making croissants is a thankless and laborious task and the ones you buy in patisseries are often far better. If you can't get good ones near you, then you'll find yourself with an excellent excuse to go to Rome.

Whenever we had guests for lunch at Schonortli when I was a girl, I would watch Nonno and Corrado with a welling sense of pride. They played host like beautiful actors, always making sure there was enough food on the table and that everyone's glass was full. There was an effortlessness to it which was a joy to watch, and one year when I had invited my two best friends to stay, I wanted to hug Corrado for the way he made them feel at home with plates of his favourite delicacies from home and bottles of good prosecco.

Since becoming a student I had forgotten some of those valuable lessons, choosing beans on toast and cheap cider over a good meal, or pasta which took 10 minutes to prepare and even less time to eat so I could make it to the union disco on time. But with each day that I spent in Rome I quickly rediscovered that one of the greatest lessons Italy had to teach was how to eat well. Eating is a way of life and sharing good food with friends is as important to the Italians as falling in love is to the French.

Eating became my new social life and before long my weeks were filled with dinner invitations and people offering to show me the best restaurants and bars the city had to offer. I will never forget the first dinner party I went to – there was something terribly 'grown-up' about the whole

Eating became my new social life

evening, which made me feel a little like a girl dressing up in her mother's clothes. The invitation was from a girl on my history of art course, Francesca Galeota, whose parents were abroad and had left her in charge of their antique-filled apartment. It was beautiful, understated yet elegant, with a huge balcony which we ate on. The evening was clear and warm, a starry sky lit up the city below, and I could hear the familiar sound of motorinos and cats mewing. We ate bruschetta and drank wine while Francesca told us about a recent trip she had taken to Venice with a friend. They had eaten *cicetti*, the city's version of tapas, served with thimbles of wine called *ombras*. She explained that the stallholders on market day used to sit and drink a glass of wine in the evening after work, when the setting sun cast shadows over St Mark's Square, hence the poetic name *ombra*, which means 'shade'.

Our first course was Spaghetti Aglio e Olio, a typically Roman dish made with fine, al dente spaghettini and an oil and garlic sauce, served with heaps of fresh Parmesan. There was a choice for the main course between *cotechino* – a delicious meaty Italian pork sausage, seasoned with bitter chocolate, cloves and cinnamon and served with wet polenta – and a favourite of my father's, Osso Bucco Milanese served with hot toast for the creamy marrow and saffron rice. I had a little of each, keen to sample everything, and it would be hard to choose between them, but the sausage with its chocolatey kick had the slight edge, purely for originality. The dessert was one of those divinely simple concoctions you wish you had thought of yourself. It was basically just a ganache, and Francesca had scattered crystallised rose petals around it. It was sweet, rich and irresistibly moreish and only took moments to prepare. For something similar, simply make a ganache by pouring heated cream over chocolate chunks and place it in a large heart-shaped mould to set.

It was such a beautiful evening that we all decided to go for a walk, and Francesca led the way to the Borghesi gardens. We sat on one of the walls, passing a bottle of wine round and eating amaretti that someone had brought as a dinner gift. There was a slight breeze and all we could hear was the sound of our own voices and the gentle rustling of poplar trees. That evening opened my eyes to a new kind of hospitality, which comes from the relaxed confidence of knowing what to serve and who to invite. Sitting on Francesca's balcony with a dozen other people I had never met before, I felt as though I belonged: I wanted to run and phone my mother and tell her I was falling in love with Italy.

Eating well is a skill the Italians have down to a fine art. *Pranzo*, lunch, is usually the biggest meal of the day and a time when most husbands come home to eat with their families. I remember being surprised when my mother told me how Nonno used to take two hours off at lunchtime when she was little to come home and eat with them. It seemed like such a luxury to have that time during the day, but my mother says it gave him more time to find out if she hadn't been doing well at school and she sometimes became so tense she could barely eat a thing. In Rome, I learnt to take care over what I ate, shopping for fresh fruit and vegetables at the market in Campo dei Fiori and buying all my meat and fish on the day, enjoying the freedom to choose what I ate by what looked good that day, rather than having to rely on tinned and frozen food.

At the university, everyone I knew ate their big meal at around midday at one of the *mensas*, student cafeterias. I will never forget the first time a friend invited me to join him. Roberto was a small, wiry architecture student from Calabria whom everyone affectionately called Ricci ('tight curls' in Italian), because of his curly hair. He insisted I meet him and some friends at the *mensa* near my faculty in Piazza Repubblica. The only canteens I had ever eaten in back home were sorry affairs boasting a few half-stale sandwiches and some reheated pizzas, so I wasn't thrilled at the prospect – but this was different. There was a choice of three dishes – meat, fish or vegetarian – each coming with a starter and dessert. It was like being in a restaurant and everyone laughed at me for taking so long to choose what I wanted. Afterwards, we all went for a coffee at the tiny bar next door, which did excellent creamy cappuccinos and lethal espresso shots with some biscotti on the side.

Most of my friends lived with their parents on the outskirts of the city and almost all of them ate at home in the evenings before coming out again. I soon learnt that clichés were often justified in Rome, where most of the boys I knew insisted their mothers were the best cooks and if they had to eat anything else, usually preferred to cook it themselves rather than risk being poisoned by someone they didn't know. Once I had been in Rome a few weeks and was beginning to feel more sure of myself, I invited a new friend, Alessandro, to lunch. He accepted, but on the condition that he do the cooking and he made me the quickest, tastiest pasta dish with just some tinned salmon, garden peas and fresh cream. We ate it with a fork in one hand and a slice of bread in the other, just like Corrado used to eat at Schonortli, and I found myself telling him all about my family and those wonderful summer holidays with my cousins.

His family was originally from Naples, and the next time we met he drove me around Rome on the back of his motorino, weaving in and out of the traffic with heart-stopping speed. He showed me the best places to buy Neapolitan pizza and calzone, a delicious *granita di caffè* which was so strong it gave me palpitations for the rest of the day, and a Torta Pasqualina like the one my mother used to eat at Easter with her family. He bought me a box of Sicilian *cannoli* made with fresh ricotta and bitter chocolate, and a creamy slab of semifreddo. We found it in a small *pasticceria* near the Pantheon, sold in rectangular chunks and made with roasted almonds, pistachios, dark chocolate and honey. It tasted a little like a soft version of Corrado's chocolate salami and we ate it outside the shop before it had time to melt.

It was getting dark by the time we had finished our shopping and we went to the Forum to eat, climbing to the monument to the Vestal Virgins, the site of their temple, which stands next to a tranquil lily pond. By the time we were ready to go it was dark, and we walked down to the Colosseum and then drove back through the city. Some of my friends told me how they often scaled the gates to the Forum late at night and sat there drinking wine under the stars, a romantic way to enjoy a romantic city and the best way I know of making the most of a glass of wine.

I learnt more in Rome than I ever dreamed I would and came away feeling a great sense of pride in my Italian heritage. I came back with a new vocabulary of words, an address book full of numbers and a recipe folder bulging at the seams with new dishes. But the best of those was the one for the bitter chocolate semifreddo I had that day with Alessandro, and every time I make it I think of the Forum at night and feel a haunting, ancient sadness wash over me.

BITTER CHOCOLATE, NUT & HONEY SEMIFREDDO

450 ml (16 fl oz) whipping cream
1 vanilla pod, split lengthways
100 g (3½ oz) dark chocolate, chopped
2 tablespoons clear honey
100 g (3½ oz) caramelised almonds (page 31), crushed
4 eggs, separated
50 g (1¾ oz) caster sugar

Place the cream in a bowl with the vanilla pod and allow to infuse for about 30 minutes. Sieve and leave to one side.

Melt the chocolate with the honey, add the nuts and allow to cool.

Whisk the egg yolks with the sugar until light and creamy. In a separate bowl, whip the cream until stiff and, in another bowl again, whisk the egg whites to form stiff peaks.

Gently mix everything together and pour into a loaf tin. Cover with clingfilm and freeze. Remove about 30 minutes before you are ready to eat and serve in thin slices.

Serves 8–10

CHAPTER 19:

In Search of Chocolate

*E*ating chocolate, for me, has always been special. It reminds me of family when I'm far away, and fills me with a warm glow when I can share it with the people I love. It was chocolate which bound me to my mother – giving me the same pleasure it had given her when she was a girl – and the recipes I have from that time are among my most treasured. But there is a joy in discovering things for yourself too. I felt that in Paris and Rome, when I still had so much to prove and wanted desperately to deserve my independence. And yet I found that the further I went from home, the closer to it I felt, as though cooking and eating well brought me back to my roots and gave me an even greater sense of pride in my family.

But nothing has been more of a discovery than marrying and having children of my own. Never had I needed those old traditions and that new spirit of independence to meet more than when I left for my honeymoon, or set off for a new life in Australia - feeling a little like a snail, carrying my whole world on my shoulders and heading off into the unknown. But I found in my husband a fellow adventurer – a teacher, a guide and a best friend. The joy of sharing new things with him is unrivalled and the lessons he has taught me about love, loyalty and friendship have made me understand how Nonno and my mother could give up so much for the men they loved.

Truly exceptional meals are few and far between, while chocolate, with its rich heritage and easy charm, is never a disappointment

I remember sharing an *assiette du fromage* and a bottle of rough house wine with my husband in Venice, enjoying the familiar warmth of our small osteria and listening to the soft lapping of the boats in the lagoon outside. That was certainly memorable, as was the Korean barbecue we had in Laos, watching the geckos dart across the ceiling above us, or the hot Thai green curry we ate in the gutter in Bangkok, lifting our feet several inches off the ground to avoid the cockroaches. They each gave us something, helped us grow and showed us that there is a world out there to discover and explore. The taste of a fresh, warm baguette with runny fried eggs and hot chilli from a street stall in Hanoi, or a plate of barbecued Balmain bugs on a beach in Sydney, made us smile with self-congratulatory pride – we were broadening our horizons, learning about life, and it felt good to push the boundaries and venture away from what we knew was safe.

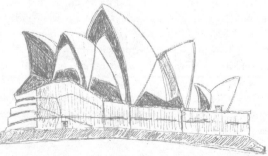

Sydney Opera House

Truly exceptional meals are few and far between, while chocolate, with its rich heritage and easy charm, is never a disappointment. We found new chocolate too, my husband and I, searching for it in Paris on our last stop before coming home after nearly a year away. The shop was on Rue Fontaine and was just like one of those cake shops I used to visit in Berne as a child. It was adorned with boxes of traditional bonbons, pastries, fudge, and so much chocolate I didn't know where to look first. The owner, Denise Acabo, was a true eccentric and as I eyed her generous selection of delicacies, I felt an urge to run and hug her. She wore her chestnut hair in plaits and drew us in with a mischievous smile and an insistent push. We must have spent at least an hour browsing the shelves – sampling dark chocolate tablets from Rheims, chocolate mints from Nice, and delicious, soft-centred eclairs made by nuns and served in little blue and white tin boxes. We left with gifts for everyone and that innocent joy sweet things bring.

Still, nothing will ever taste as good as Omama's biscuits, made by my mother and myself, eaten in front of the Christmas tree at home with all the people I love around me, or a slice of Nonna's Napoleon's Torte on my birthday, still warm from the oven. I remember dreaming of chocolate when I was in Asia, tasting it almost and willing myself to be at home with my mother, sharing a pot of Omama's Chocolate Mousse or a slice of roulade.

Now I find myself at the other end of the world, nostalgic, lonely sometimes, and missing home, but as Christmas approaches and I begin to think about making Omama's chocolate spice biscuits, I know I will be all right.

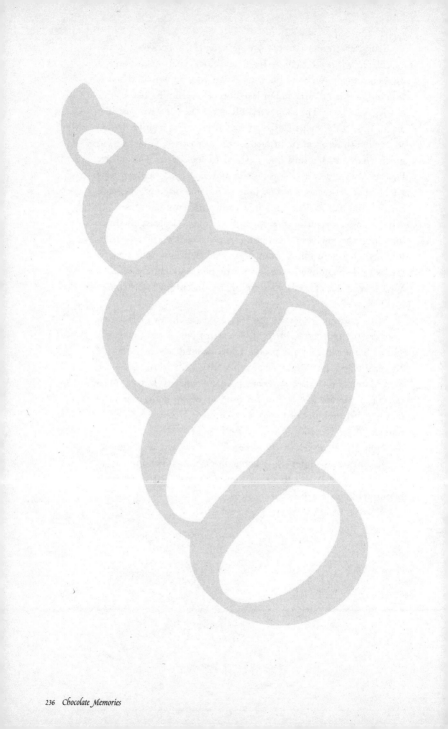

Glossary

Babbo: Italian for father

Buon appetito: Italian for 'good appetite'

Buongiorno: Italian for good morning

Buona notte: Italian for good night

Cucina: Italian for kitchen

Fornaio: Italian for bakery

Grazie altre tanto: traditional Italian response to 'buon appetito', meaning 'and to all of you'

Haxihus: Swiss German for outside playhouse

La dolce vita: the sweet life; 'dolce' also means a sweet or dessert in Italian

Linden: the lime-trees down by the berry orchard in Schonortli

Madrina: Italian for godmother

Mama: Italian for mother

Nonna: Italian for grandmother

Nonno: Italian for grandfather

Omama: Swiss German for grandmother

Opapa: Swiss German for grandfather

Pasqua: Italian for Easter

Sala: Italian for dining room

Salotto: Italian for living room

Schonortli: my grandparents' holiday home on the lake of Thun in Switzerland

Schwartz Peter: Swiss card game about a chimney sweep

Scopa: Italian card game

Spielzimmer: Swiss German for playroom

St Nicholas's Day: festival held on 6 December when children leave their slippers out for St Nicholas to fill with chocolates

Tabaccheria: Italian for a tobacconist's shop

Tante: Swiss German for aunt
Vincoli: Italian for narrow alleyways
Zia: Italian for aunt
Zio: Italian for uncle

CULINARY TERMS

Bain-marie: method of melting chococolate in a bowl over a pan
  of simmering water
Biscotti: twice-baked crunchy Italian biscuits, often flavoured
  with hazelnuts or almonds
Cailler: Swiss brand of chococolate
Cannoli: Italian dessert consisting of deep-fried pastry shells
  filled with ricotta
'Carta della musica' dough: very thin pastry
Chalah: plaited egg bread
Chocolat ancien: a very rich version of hot chocolate with
  melted dark chocolate and hot milk
Chocolat chaud: French version of hot chocolate
Cioccolata Fiorentina: Italian version of hot chocolate
Colomba: Easter panettone shaped like a dove and topped with
  sugar crystals
Contorno: Italian for a side dish
Couverture: cooking chococolate
Crostini: small slices of toasted bread
Ganache: a mixture of chocolate and cream for filling and
  coating desserts
Gefilte fish: chopped herring
Glühwein: mulled wine
Granita: Italian drink made with crushed ice and flavourings
Guezi: Swiss German for biscuits
Hernli: a Swiss version of macaroni cheese
Honigleckerli: Swiss German honeyed spice bread
Kuchen: Swiss German for tart
Lebkuchen: a thick cake-like biscuit, flavoured with honey,
  lemon, spices and almonds and coated with a hard sugar glaze
Mandelmailanderli: Swiss German almond biscuits
Marquise: a glazed dessert, halfway between a chocolate mousse
  and a parfait

Menier: dark cooking chococolate

Merenda: Italian version of a teatime snack

Mirtilli: Italian for bilberries

Napoleon's Torte: dense chocolate cake made with ground almonds and breadcrumbs

Pain d'épices: spiced bread or gingerbread

Pane rustica: Italian table bread or coarse bread

Panettone: Italian festival bread made with currants and candied peel

Panforte: Italian honey cake made with nuts and candied pumpkin

Panpepato: Italian spice bread made with black pepper from which panforte originates

Raclette: a dish of melted raclette cheese

Ragu: a classic Italian meat sauce

Rhue bread: rye bread

Risotto Milanese: risotto flavoured with saffron, white wine and beef marrow

Spitzbuben: Swiss German Christmas biscuits – vanilla sandwiches filled with redcurrant jam

Sugo: tomato sauce

Tempering: the prococess of heating and cooling chococolate to give it a gloss and a snap

Torrone: nougat

Torta di Nonna: literally Grandmother's Tart, usually made with pine nuts, almonds and lemon zest

Vanillepretzel: Swiss German vanilla biscuits

Weggli: Swiss egg-glazed bread rolls

Weinacht Guezi: Swiss German for Christmas biscuits

Wurstel: Swiss sausages for roasting over a fire

Zabaglione: an Italian dessert made by whisking egg yolks, Marsala and sugar over simmering water

Zimt Sterne: Swiss German star biscuits to hang from the Christmas tree

Zucca: candied pumpkin. It can be a little tricky to get hold of, but try specialist cake shops or Turkish shops around Christmas.

Zuccotto: Italian cake made with whipped cream, chococolate and candied fruit

$\mathcal{N}$otes on Cooking with Chocolate

TEMPERING CHOCOLATE

Tempering is just a fancy name for the process of melting, cooling and reheating chocolate to give it that gloss and hard snap you need for gift chocolates or for coating fruit and orange peel. I use the following method when I have time, but I also sometimes cheat and simply melt the chocolate in a bain-marie, set the bowl in a sink of cold water for a few moments and then return it to the heat briefly and I find it works just as well. If you want to make sure you get it right, here is the professional version.

Break the chocolate into small chunks and place in a bain-marie over a low heat. Stir often until the chocolate has reached around 45°C (115°F) on a sugar thermometer. Then remove the bowl and cool in a sink filled with cold water. When the temperature has dropped to 25°C (75°F), return the bowl to the simmering bain-marie and heat, stirring well, until the temperature rises again to 30°C (85°F).

If you are adding spices or flavourings, do so at the last stage, just before heating the chocolate for the second time.

BUYING AND STORING CHOCOLATE

When selecting chocolate, try not to be intimidated by the choice. There are so many famous names, each one purporting to be the best. I have used Lindt, Menier and Valhrona and all three are excellent for both cooking and tempering, but I am sure cheaper supermarket brands will do just as well as long as you look out for the following. Don't choose chocolate which has white streaks or marbling. This is called chocolate or fat bloom and although it doesn't affect the taste too much, it can give it a crumbly texture rather than the desired sharp snap. It is caused by the cocoa butter separating and rising to the surface and you sometimes get it if you keep your chocolate too warm or damp.

Chocolate is a delicate creature. Store it in a cool dry place, at around 15°C (60°F), with less than 50 per cent humidity. It tends to absorb other odours easily so store it away from anything with a strong smell. You can keep good-quality dark chocolate indefinitely at the right temperature – assuming you have enormous self-control – but white and milk chocolate should not be kept for more than 10 months because of their milk solids.

MAKING FLAVOURED SUGARS

I learnt how to do this on holiday in La Rochelle, where my host had an entire kitchen cabinet devoted to jars of flavoured sugar. Not only do they look beautiful, but they are a great way of spicing up cakes and biscuits and are much cheaper than the varieties you can buy in the shops.

VANILLA SUGAR

There are several ways of doing this. One way is to scoop out the pulp from one or two vanilla pods and blend them in a food processor with the sugar. But I simply split three pods lengthways and place them in an airtight jar of caster sugar. After three days the sugar will be ready to use and you can store it pretty much indefinitely. I use this in Omama's Vanillepretzel and once added it to a rich chocolate loaf cake which I served warm with some fresh ricotta and honey.

CINNAMON SUGAR

Place two sticks of cinnamon in a jar of caster sugar and add a few tablespoons of ground cinnamon. Leave it to infuse for about a week. It is lovely in Christmas biscuits and festive cakes and breads. Try sprinkling some on top of a slice of raisin bread and toasting it under the grill.

Anything containing dark chocolate and cardamom is at the height of culinary fashion at the moment. Cardamom sugar is one of those things which sounds exotic and really couldn't be simpler. But there is a catch: cardamom has a very distinctive taste and I have often found it too overpowering in desserts, so use it sparingly. I peel and crush about six black cardamom pods into a large jar of caster sugar and leave for three days for the flavour to infuse properly. Use it in rich dark chocolate Tortes and chocolate crème brûlée and try not to sound too smug.

CAKE DECORATION IDEAS

I have spent hours deliberating over whether to scatter crystallised petals or candied peel on top of chocolate cakes in the past and still don't know which I prefer. I can't tell you how to make a professional-looking white royal icing with frills and flowers for a wedding cake, my patience simply doesn't last that long, but I have discovered some delightful and simple ways of making basic cake recipes look shop-bought.

Never underestimate the beauty of icing sugar. I once made a sticky orange and almond cake and a chocolate cardamom sponge for a Moroccan-themed party and sprinkled them with sifted icing sugar; I received the nicest compliments for both. Dark chocolate, flourless cakes look wonderful with some icing sugar and a few crystallised lilac petals scattered on top.

For an anniversary or Valentine's Day treat, cut your chocolate cake into a heart shape and place a ball of white-chocolate ganache in the centre. Make some chocolate caramel shapes and sprinkle with edible gold leaf, then stick one or two in the ganache. The effect is quite magical and really very simple to do.

Spice up a lemon cake with dark chocolate caramel hearts, stuck roughly into the top of the cake, and sprinkle with edible gold dust. For a child's birthday cake, cover a chocolate sponge with white butter icing and sprinkle liberally with silver sugar balls. My favourite decoration for chocolates and pieces of torrone or panforte is to pour tempered dark chocolate all over and then place tiny slivers of pistachio nut, candied orange peel and dried fig on top.

Enjoy experimenting, and remember – if it doesn't come out quite as you expected, you can always eat the trials.

Index

The index is arranged in word-by-word order. Page numbers for the illustrations and recipe titles are shown in *italics*.